Lectionary Tales
For The Pulpit

Series III
Cycle A

Constance Berg

CSS Publishing Company, Inc., Lima, Ohio

Copyright © 2001 by
CSS Publishing Company, Inc.
Lima, Ohio

Scripture quotations, unless marked otherwise, are from the *New Revised Standard Version of the Bible*, copyright 1989 by the Division of Christian Education of the National Council of the Churches of Christ in the USA. Used by permission.

Library of Congress Cataloging-in-Publication Data

Berg, Constance, 1959-
    Lectionary tales for the pulpit. Series III. Cycle A / Constance Berg.
      p.   cm.
    ISBN 0-7880-1815-9 (alk. paper)
    1. Lectionary preaching. 2. Homiletical illustrations. I. Title.
BV4235.L43 B46   2001
252'.6—dc21   2001025087
                                                        CIP

For more information about CSS Publishing Company resources, visit our website at www.csspub.com.

ISBN 0-7880-1815-9

I dedicate this work to the glory of God. God has richly blessed me as I hear people's stories and as I have looked back over my own life. As a writer and personal historian, I see over and over again that there is no such thing as an "ordinary" person. Every person I meet has a wonderful story (or two, or three!) to tell how God works in his or her life. I hear how seemingly "ordinary" things point to God's unfailing love. I hear about miracles that happen when there was no hope left. I am convinced that God uses us as we are. God blesses us wherever we are on our faith journey.

I dedicate this book once again to my very supportive family: my husband David; my children Kjrstin and Andrew. Thanks, Kjrstin, for reading my stories and being so enthusiastic about them — even at the age of ten! Thanks, Andrew, for your strong hugs. I love you three more than I can ever say!

And to my extended family: my parents, Dick and Hetty Doesburg, who support me and listen to all my stories and thoughts. Thanks for always being there for me! And to Leno and Phyllis Berg for being the nicest in-laws!

I also want to thank my sister, Ingrid Doesburg Munsterman, my best friend for 41 years. When we were very young we shared a bedroom and Ingrid never minded telling me stories. She'd make up stories every night — some funny, some like folk lore, and some very wild. I am convinced that she has helped expand my thinking process with her most imaginative stories. Her students are very fortunate to have someone with such a creative mind! Thanks, Ing — I love you!

Lastly, thanks to CSS Publishing for the wonderful opportunity to share people's stories. Thank you, Pastor Wes Runk, Tom Lentz, and Terry Rhoads!

Constance Doesburg Berg
Grand Forks, North Dakota

Table Of Contents

Preface

This is the last of the three books I was invited to write for the *Lectionary Tales For The Pulpit* series. What a joy it has been to be able to cover the whole lectionary cycle! I wish the reader many blessings while reading the stories. It is my hope that the stories of ordinary, real people will touch you as their experiences help illustrate God working in their lives.

Candlelight At Advent

*" 'Therefore you also must be ready, for the Son of Man
is coming at an unexpected hour.' " (v. 44)*

The church year is dictated not by a fiscal or chronological calendar, but a religious calendar that revolves around the events of the life of Christ. Since the sixth or seventh century, the first day of the church year begins with the first Sunday of Advent, which means "arrival." As Christians, we anticipate the arrival of baby Jesus.

Advent begins an exciting time of anticipation to the celebration of the birth of Christ. Children especially love the symbols of the Advent season of the church. Many churches light the Advent candles, one by one, as a "countdown" toward Christmas.

Some churches use four blue (which stands for royalty and signifies hope), purple (for wealth), or white (for the purity of Jesus Christ) candles. Many use three white and one pink (for joy) candle. Still others use a combination of colors. However it is done, there are four candles used for the four Sundays that lead up to the Nativity of Our Lord.

The first candle is the Prophecy Candle, used to remind us that God has promised to rebuild broken lives and give us spiritual prosperity. The Prophecy Candle is lit to help us recall God's never-ending love and grace.

The second candle, the Bethlehem Candle, reminds us that Jesus could have been born in a palace with royal appointments all around. He could have been born in regal splendor. He could have had a bed of purple silk or velvet, the costliest of all fabrics, a sign of royalty and immeasurable wealth. Instead, God uses ordinary elements and ordinary people. Jesus was born in the small town of Bethlehem, in a barn, in a manger filled with hay, wrapped in rags.

The Shepherd's Candle comes in the third week of Advent, pointing to the Supreme Shepherd in Jesus Christ. As sheep need a shepherd, so we need Jesus to guide us, to care for us, and to watch over us.

The Angel Candle, the last candle, reminds us that the angel of the Lord said, "Do not be afraid for I bring you good tidings of great joy." We need not fear the unknown or the future. God looks upon us with love, grace, and mercy.

Four candles, four Sundays, four weeks of anticipation. Four points to ponder as each candle lights our way in our journey of reflection this Advent season. May each candle light something within you as you experience God's gift of Jesus Christ.

The Viking Bachelor

"May the God of hope fill you with all joy and peace in believing, so that you may abound in hope by the power of the Holy Spirit." (v. 13)

In 1948 there lived a group of bachelors in the small Minnesota town of Viking. There were one hundred single men in Viking. There was one single woman.

The pastor, Rev. C. T. Thompson, held parties for the men and they spent time picnicking, hunting, and fishing. He even had dinners for the men, who ranged from 21 to 81. He wanted these men from Zion Lutheran Church to make the best of their bachelorhood.

On February 29 of that year, a group at Honeywell in Minneapolis brought their secretary, Ruth Peterson, a newspaper report of this town and their bachelors. She was intrigued. The headline read: "Leap Year Lure: Single Men of Viking Outnumber Women 100 to 1." Ruth was taking night classes in Swedish and business. She wasn't dating anyone in particular, and her friends thought it would be good for her to read it. They convinced her to write the pastor for names of eligible bachelors. She received LeRoy Sustad's name.

Pastor Thompson, who never married, was successful in getting many of the bachelors married off. Unfortunately, LeRoy was related to most of the girls around Viking. Pastor Thompson knew LeRoy would have to be introduced to a girl who was not a local. How lucky that a young lady wanted a name!

Ruth wrote LeRoy a letter, telling him about her life in Akeley and her work at Honeywell. She told him about her night courses in business and Swedish. She mentioned that she was skeptical of writing to a stranger, but she did request an answer. On the envelope she wrote her vital statistics: 5'5", 135 pounds, dark blonde hair, blue eyes.

Ruth didn't get a letter from LeRoy. His mother, Tillie, wrote Ruth explaining that LeRoy was very sick with scarlet fever but that he would write as soon as he could. "LeRoy got your letter yesterday and he was surprised and tickled to get it. LeRoy is sick and he would love more letters."

So Ruth kept on writing. Finally in March, LeRoy wrote to Ruth. He was feeling much better. Then a few days later he wrote again and included a photograph of himself. Letters kept coming and they decided to meet in May when LeRoy was coming to Minneapolis for his brother, Orville's, graduation from Bethel College. He joked that he could find Ruth's rooming place because he had a spotlight on his Chevrolet Coupe.

Ruth was very excited to meet him. They met on May 23, 1948, when LeRoy came to pick Ruth up for the graduation. The next day they went to an amusement park. They rode the Ferris wheel and ate at Hasty Tasty. Later they went for a picnic at a lake. Ruth found it hard to say good-bye.

LeRoy wrote again, thanking her and mentioning he was honored she thought of him — and to think he was Swedish! He said she was a real "honey." On the fourth of July weekend, Ruth rode a bus all the way from Minneapolis to Thief River Falls, where LeRoy picked her up to meet his parents, Tillie and Henry. He proposed on July 3.

Ruth was ecstatic. Was this the right step for her? She had been praying about it for some time. She wanted to do what was right. She wanted to obey God's will. Her evening devotion was Psalm 118:23. "This is the Lord's doing and it is marvelous in our eyes." At that moment, she had nothing to fear. She felt the Lord was leading her and LeRoy in their journey together. She agreed to marry him.

They saw each other for Thanksgiving and Christmas. They were married on June 15, 1949. After their wedding at First Covenant Church, LeRoy swept his bride away in his 1938 Chevrolet Coupe. They returned from their honeymoon to a new farm. LeRoy also spent 22 years on the Soo Line Railroad. Ruth worked for Arctic Cat. "We were busy with church activities," Ruth added, "and we had cattle, chickens, pigs, and sheep." Together they reared a son and a daughter.

Today, Ruth and LeRoy Sustad have been married more than fifty years and enjoy their six grandchildren and six great-grandchildren. They have been asked several times as to what they attribute the success of their marriage. LeRoy says they have no big secrets from each other. "Two shall become as one." They get along.

In the Sustad dining room hangs a wooden plaque with just one word, "DATSUS." "It's our name backwards," Ruth laughs. "Dat's us." All around the plaque are the words, "love, joy, peace, patience, kindness, goodness, faithfulness, self-control," something these two have practiced on one another for more than half a century.

Ruth reminds LeRoy that their daily morning devotions and trust in the Lord for whatever comes is the basis for taking one day at a time and thanking God for it. For where there is love and the spirit of God there is patience, kindness, joy, peace, goodness, faithfulness, self-control.

(Based on a story by Naomi Dunavan in the Sunday, June 13, 1999 issue of the Grand Forks (ND) *Herald*.)

A Great Prophet And A Great Dad

" 'Truly I tell you, among those born of women no one has arisen greater than John the Baptist; yet the least in the kingdom of heaven is greater than he.' " (v. 11)

John the Baptist was the real thing, a great prophet. He would never see Jesus be crucified or even be resurrected. John would be executed by then. Still, John the Baptist prepares the way and is a zealot in his ministry.

Dick was the real thing, a true family man. He knew he was not immortal; he would not be able to be with his children forever. He couldn't know what the future held for them. He just knew he loved his family and would do whatever he could for them. He also knew they were loved by God.

John the Baptist loved Jesus. He did not mind wearing a robe of camel's hair. He did not mind eating locusts. He could endure difficulties for the sake of his beliefs.

Dick loved his children. He did not mind living sparingly. He did not mind foregoing fancy things or passing up overtime at work in favor of spending time with his children. He was glad to live a simple life for their sake.

John the Baptist prepared the way for Jesus's coming. He preached around the time Jesus began his ministry. He insisted the Jews

be immersed in the baptism as a sign of repentance. Just like the Gentiles. They were on equal footing to face judgment.

Dick gave his children a solid foundation. There were plenty of church activities for the children to go to. Friends abounded both at school and in the neighborhood. Heavily involved in the homeless mission and Habitat for Humanity, the family took on an active role in the community. He insisted they become involved in social outreach. He wanted them to be aware of suffering and understand the ways of the world.

Jesus held his cousin, John the Baptist, in high regard. John was one of the greatest prophets. Jesus also knew there were greater ones to come with the beginning of the age of salvation. For Jesus, there was none greater than John the Baptist, who prepared the way.

Jesus holds Dick in high regard. Dick is a wonderful father. His children will also be excellent parents due to Dick's example, and, according to Dick's children, their dad is the best.

Angels Among Us

"... an angel of the Lord appeared to him in a dream and said, 'Joseph, son of David, do not be afraid to take Mary as your wife, for the child conceived in her is from the Holy Spirit....' " (v. 20)

Books and magazines are filled with people's encounters with "angels": people who give selflessly, people who practice random acts of kindness, people who give without wanting or expecting anything in return. There is no doubt that there are angels among us. Almost everyone has a story about something a person has done for him or her without motive, through kindness and grace. But not many people can say they have been visited by an angelic being, as is the biblical account of Joseph's visit from the angel.

In ancient times, angels were considered to be supernatural, spiritual messengers or beings who did God's will on earth. Angels were a promised form of communication with God. Angels came to speak to people in the Bible; they had a specific message for the person. It could be counsel, clarification, or a divine warning. Joseph's angel came to give clarity to the situation of Mary's pregnancy. Sometimes an angel's message was one of pure joy, as when the shepherds saw a group of angels singing in jubilant chorus to announce the arrival of the baby Jesus (Luke 2:13-14). Sometimes the message was foreboding, and the angel would give a warning, as in the case of Joseph having to flee Egypt with Mary and the infant Jesus (Matthew 2:13). Sometimes they were helpful, as when an angel protected the fleeing Israelites by placing a pillar of clouds between them and the Egyptians (Exodus 14:19-20). One angel slaughtered 185,000 Assyrians for trying to attack Jerusalem (2 Kings 19:35).

The outward appearance of angels is hardly given notice. It was their function that was of importance in the Scriptures. They were usually recognized immediately, either as being perceived as God or as being clothed in garments that made them seem heavenly, such as a white robe, or a being bathed in bright light.

In contrast, appearance is of major importance in the modern world. Today's versions of angels are little knickknacks that sit on a shelf, or little pins that sit on our shoulders, or even statues to whom people bring flowers. We tend to adore these little interpretations of angels. We have cute poems and easily call people — family and friends alike — "angels." Angelic beings come in every ethnic color, every pose conceivable, and every dress imaginable and are made of every material imaginable: plastic, ceramic, porcelain, and so on.

Angels are considered a reminder of things dear and sweet. My son has a little angel ornament dressed in a hockey uniform that we hang on our Christmas tree. There are even angels dressed in ballerina tutus and aprons and chef's hats. An angel adorns our wall, holding a watering can and spade, wearing a wide-brimmed hat. She wears gardening gloves and wears a little sign that says "gardening angel." A little magnet on my refrigerator reads: "God in His love often sends His gift of angels — we call them 'friends.' "

Angels are definitely among us. We know that when we use a much broader definition of "angel": a nurse who sits with us in the recovery room, making sure we are okay after major surgery; a feeling that overcomes us and causes us to stop on the side of the road which in turn saves our lives as we watch a tire blow out; a neighbor who will sit for hours making silk flower pieces for a wedding because the florist's order is mistakenly canceled; a sixth sense, if you will, not to trust something that turns out to be evil and sinister. Divine messages come in many forms.

Angels come in many forms. Have you ever been considered an angel?

The Reason For The Season

"On entering the house, they saw the child with Mary his mother; and they knelt down and paid him homage." (v. 8)

Aunt Carla is adamant about her celebration of Christmas. It can only be one way. Every detail has to focus on the birth of Jesus. No beautiful photos of deer grazing in the woods. Snow-covered valleys or cabins do nothing for her; it's not unusual to have six feet of snow on the ground by Christmas where she lives. She will pass up the cards with Santa, reindeer, and elves all happily engaging in the business of gift-giving. She has enough trouble buying, buying, buying. She doesn't want to be reminded that it's an expensive holiday. Instead she focuses on cards that show the true meaning of Christmas: ones with a nativity scene on it perhaps. A baby in a manger. Something that reminds her of what the first Christmas must have been like. Ornaments and gifts reflect Christmas and the true meaning of Christmas for her: the birth of Jesus.

Aunt Carla's home reflects the holiday: chrismons adorn her tree; candles illuminate a nativity scene on the mantel and cards include gifts of sponsorship to charities and schools. Aunt Carla's life, for that matter, reflects the true meaning of Christmas as she takes in those who need help. Every Christmas has another group of people at her home: friends, family, and others who don't have a place to go. Her whole life has been directed toward others: helping, teaching, and sharing. Aunt Carla knows the true meaning of Christmas.

So Unnecessary!

"A voice was heard in Ramah, wailing and loud lamentation, Rachel weeping for her children; she refused to be consoled, because they are no more." (v. 18)

Some things are beyond understanding — especially when a loss of life is preventable. Especially when it involves a life just beginning.

Mary had twins. Her first son was delivered but her stomach was unusually large. The doctor suspected she was having another. The other twin came 53 minutes later. But it was too late. They didn't know he was coming. He died in the birth process. So tragic!

Kathy also had twins. They knew twins were coming, and Kathy, her husband, and the doctors were prepared. The birth was uneventful and she took home two cute little girls. At six months one could see that they didn't look alike — they were fraternal twins. Ashley had brown hair, was short, and was the spitting image of her dad. Kaitlyn had blond hair and was long and lean like her mother. She looked like a miniature Kathy. One night Kathy came to check on the girls, only to find that Kaitlyn lay in her end of the crib, dead. They suspected Sudden Infant Death Syndrome, but they will never know what killed her. So unnecessary!

Henry was driving his children to school when his truck slid on a patch of ice. He was wearing his seat belt and was unhurt. His three children, riding unbelted in the front of the truck, were thrown out the front window. They died instantly. Three minutes. Three lives extinguished. It was something that could have been prevented.

Cheryl and Debbie were chatting at the kitchen table while the children were swimming in the pool. Their two-year-olds were out back playing in the dirt. Or that's what they thought. Debbie's oldest screamed, and she and Cheryl came running. The two-year-olds had fallen in the water and in all the noise and excitement, the older children didn't notice. They had drowned. What a pity. What a waste.

Some things are beyond understanding. They defy explanation. They are so unnecessary.

Grace Upon Grace

"From his fullness we have all received grace upon grace." (v. 16)

Laura Fischer is growing up to be a lovely young lady. She is an example of grace and perseverance. Why? Read what this tenth-grader wrote in a school essay after a trip she took with her church group:

"During the long ride into Minnesota, I occupied my time with watching the mountains rise up from the powdery white earth. It was a perfect day. The sky was completely clear and the sun reflected brightly off the snow. We pulled onto the road that would lead us to Lustern Mountains. There were people everywhere. All of the local people had decided to go skiing that day because of the beautiful weather.

"I was in the rental office when I discovered that most of the resort's equipment had already been rented out, so I decided to try snowboarding. I was assigned a deep blue board with step-in bindings. I thought that it was very nice, and I couldn't wait to get out on the slopes and try it out. First, however, I put the board down on the lodge carpet and snapped my boots into the bindings. I leaned first one way, and then to the other, practicing my turns. I leaned to the left, then to the right feeling more confident, and suddenly I fell over and discovered just how hard getting up after taking a spill would be.

"It didn't discourage me, though. I quickly scrambled to my feet and headed straight for the bunny hill. Grabbing hold of the towrope, I pulled myself to the top of the small hill on unsteady legs. Standing nervously at the top of the hill, my heart began to pound. With a surge of adrenaline, I began to slide down the hill. At first, I slid a few feet, and then I fell. I got up, and promptly fell again. After about five or six tumbles, I was finally at the bottom of the bunny hill.

"My dignity completely gone, I decided to try it again — you can't start out as a pro, can you? So, once again, I latched onto the towrope and hauled myself back up to the top of the hill. This time, I was a lot more cautious and I did a tiny bit better. My first day of snowboarding went on like this, with me going up and down the bunny hill. When it was time to go, I had almost mastered this tiny hill. Looking at a map of the park, I spotted a run called Big Bunny Run, so I made a mental note to check it out the next day.

"The next morning I could hardly move. I felt about as flexible as an iron pole. I was stiff and sore from head to toe. I was also ready to get back on my snowboard. I had promised myself that I would learn to snowboard, and I had my mind set on trying the Big Bunny Run.

"We got to the resort exactly at opening time. I could have gotten skis, but I had promised myself that I would stick it out with my beautiful, deep blue snowboard. I put on my boots and snapped them into my bindings. The only difference from the day before was that this day I was alone. Yesterday, other beginners had come to the little bunny hill and tried to snowboard, too. On this day, everyone had gotten skis and they were already zooming down the more difficult runs. I was alone in my effort, but I was feeling especially confident that day.

"I proudly rode the chair lift to the top of an enormous hill. I stood at the top looking down for a long time. I wondered if it had been a mistake to try to go down this hill. I gave myself a mental shake, reminding myself of my promise to learn, and soon I was down the slope. There was only one problem ... I was sliding down on my hip. Quite embarrassed, I stood up, shook the snow out of my hair, and got back on the chair lift. This time I knew what to expect and I seemed to make it a little farther than I did before. I made it almost a fourth of the way down before adding another bruise to my already battered body.

"As the day wore on, I felt myself improving. I made it almost all of the way down the hill once. I knew that it was getting late, though, and that soon I would have to stop. I would put all of my dwindling strength and concentration into my last run. I rode up the chair lift, and gave myself a pep talk. I reached the top of the hill and took a deep breath, knowing that if I thought about what I was about to do too much, I would fail. I pushed off and slid expertly down. I turned left, then right. I checked my speed, slowing almost to a stop, then let myself go faster and faster. I sped right up to the lodge, and stopped. I unsnapped my boots from the step-in bindings, and I knew that I had done it. I made it down the mountain!

"I was sore and exhausted, but I was filled with pride. I was so proud that I thought that I might burst, right there in front of everyone. As I returned the rented board, the deep blue board with step-in bindings, I felt as though I was turning in a friend that I would never see again. I took the boots off with care because I was very sore. I put my shoes on and limped back to the lodge to wait for everyone to come back. I had never worked so hard, and I was ready to go home.

"The next day was a school day. It was a very long day. I ached all over, and I was so tired that I found it very hard to concentrate. It had been worth it, though. I proved to myself that I am a very strong-willed person. When everyone else gave up, I kept trying. I had succeeded where others had failed. Of course, I still wasn't the best snowboarder but I could hold my head up high and show off my now purple bruises with pride because I had won."

Ah, such grace!

Epiphany: A Wonderful Holiday

*"When they saw that the star had stopped, they were
overwhelmed with joy." (v. 10)*

I have lived in two different countries where Epiphany is a
very important holiday: The Netherlands (where I was born) and
Mexico (where I studied, worked, and traveled). Both countries
celebrate by giving gifts between December 25 and January 6, the
day of Epiphany. What fun for children!

Epiphany is the day of the visit of the Magi to the baby Jesus,
the day that completes the twelve days of Christmas, the day when
we celebrate the Light of the world (Jesus) being born. Jesus was
born to be the Light of the world, not just the world of Bethlehem
or the Middle East, but the whole world. Jesus' birth is the mani-
festation of God's love for the entire world, not just my little world.
When we internalize all that this means, we, as Christians, react
out of love and reach out to others in need. This is a great time in
the church year to emphasize missions and social justice. Christ is
the spiritual Light of all nations, not just our nation.

And who comes to see the Light of the world but the Magi, the
wise men who follow the star. The Magi were members of a religion that believed in astrology and had at its head two gods: the
god of evil and the god of goodness. We can assume they were
wealthy: How else could they have brought such expensive gifts?
They were very learned and were of an exclusive group. The Magi
interpreted dreams and incorporated magic in their divinations. They
based their interpretation of human affairs on the alignment of the
stars. Astrology was very important to them. Just think, the wise
men found our Savior by using astrology!

Yes, even pagans such as the Magi came to adore Jesus. How
much more can we, those who have heard the good news, adore Jesus?

Baptism By Spit

"John would have prevented him, saying, 'I need to be baptized by you, and you come to me?' But Jesus answered him, 'Let it be so now; for it is proper for us in this way to fulfill all righteousness.' Then he consented." (vv. 14-15)

"Jan wasn't baptized by the spirit, she was baptized by spit," went the joke. Jan had heard it all before: the taunting and teasing from her aunts and uncles. Sure, they hadn't been there at her birth, but they loved to tell the story. They were telling Jan's friends about that fateful day when Jan was born — and baptized.

Jan's mother, Donna, was 27 weeks pregnant when the car she was driving was hit by a truck. The driver didn't see Donna's car and neither he nor Donna had time to react. The truck driver wasn't wearing a seat belt and was killed instantly. Donna's growing belly kept her pinned inside her seat belt and in the car. The volunteer fire squad and paramedics worked frantically to get her out of the wreckage.

Donna was freed after almost twenty minutes and while in the ambulance her water broke. It was too late. The baby was coming. The paramedics were on the phone with the hospital doctor on call, but the ride was still almost 45 minutes long. They would have to rely on all their training and skill to help Donna and the baby. The baby, a little girl, came fast and furious. She was tiny. About three pounds in the paramedics' estimation.

The paramedics were friends with Donna and her husband. Their town was very small and everyone knew each other. Donna taught high school English and was the school newspaper advisor.

Her husband Hal worked at a nearby mine. Hal would meet them at the hospital.

The senior paramedic, Mark, was a deeply faithful man who believed that he was privileged to be an EMT and have the opportunity to help people. He taught Biology at the middle school. He was checking Donna's vital signs when the younger paramedic, Bill, started yelling into the phone at the doctor. The baby was blue and was not responding. Bill was trying not to panic. Mark and Bill worked on the baby together and while waiting for further instructions, Mark spit on his finger and made the sign of the cross on the baby's forehead. "I baptize you, baby, in the name of the Father, Son, and Holy Spirit. Amen." He fought to remember all the baptisms he had heard in their country church. "You have been sealed by the Holy Spirit and marked with the cross of Christ forever. Let your light so shine before others that they may see your good works ... Amen." He couldn't think of the rest. "God bless you, baby girl. Amen."

Later he told Donna he didn't know why, but the feeling came over him that the baby should be baptized. There was such a good chance the baby was going to die and this might give Donna a tiny ray of hope if she did die.

The baby was revived and remained in the neonatal intensive care unit for five weeks. She was in the hospital a total of thirteen weeks while her body fought to survive and thrive. Donna and Hal, who named their baby Jan Marie, were thrilled to take her home — exactly three days after her original due date.

Jan was dedicated at church seven weeks later. The grandparents, aunts, uncles, and family from all over came to see the baby. Bill, the paramedic, was there also. But it was Mark who held the baby while the pastor symbolically poured water from the baptismal font into a shell. "The baptismal waters have already been poured on Jan when she was less than an hour old, but this water symbolizes what happened at her true baptism. Today we are reminded what happens at baptism."

The pastor had rewritten the words to accommodate Jan's former baptismal blessing given by Mark and there was not a dry eye in the congregation. Jan was baptized, Jan was a child of God, and she was a fighter!

And now, even thirty years later, Jan is still awed by what happened to her. She had always been tiny, and Mark's pet name for her was "Pipsqueak." Her dad called her "Half-pint." Her mother called her Jan.

At her son's baptism, Jan fought back tears of joy and gratitude at the thought. She was given a chance at life long ago in the ambulance. She was given the gift of the Holy Spirit at baptism.

Let them laugh at her baptism by spit. To her, it was still baptism by the Spirit!

The Love Of Being A Christian

---

*" 'He on whom you see the Spirit descend and re-
main is the one who baptizes with the Holy Spirit.
And I myself have seen and have testified that this is
the Son of God.' " (vv. 33-34)*

Bob Bohn was serving in Tan Son Nhut Air Base in Saigon,
Vietnam, in 1971. He was twenty years old and liked his job as
mechanic. He was also looking forward to going home to the States
in three months. Before his tour was complete in Vietnam, Bob
was assigned to be stationed in North Dakota. Bob had requested a
base closer to his New York home. He was thinking "closer" as in
Massachusets, New Jersey, or even New York. Not North Dakota!
He didn't know anything about North Dakota, but he made plans
to relocate to Minot Air Force Base.

A few days after he got his reassignment, Bob headed off to
call his parents from the USO club. What he saw on the way down
the stairs changed his life: baskets of letters to servicemen, organized according to state of origin. Fifty bushel baskets were filled
with letters to servicemen there in Vietnam. His curiosity was
piqued.

The young serviceman glanced at the North Dakota basket.
One caught his attention. It was simply addressed "Dear Serviceman." He opened it. The letter was written by a seventeen-year-old
girl from Bismarck, North Dakota, a town about two hours south
of Minot. She loved Spanish, animals, and horseback riding. And
she loved God. She had just dedicated her life to Christ. She ended
her letter with, "Thank you and God bless, Marlys."

Being in Vietnam had forced death to become a reality to Bob.
He had rededicated his life to Christ earlier that year after having
distanced himself from God in his teen years. "God bless," written

in loopy handwriting, caught his heart. He answered the letter to Marlys Mortvedt.

He told her what it was like teaching English and Bible classes to Vietnamese children. He shared how important it was to him now that he was a Christian to do meaningful things. "Believe me, before Christ, my life was meaningless," he wrote Marlys.

Bob felt it was worth the gamble to be honest with Marlys. "Either she'd be scared or, if anything, I'd have a date when I got to North Dakota." But Marlys wasn't scared. She wrote back within the week, saying it was great to hear from "a brother in Christ." She knew Bob was special. The two corresponded, sharing about their faith, their struggles with each of their Sunday school classes, and their Christian lives. They also shared about their dreams for the future.

Bob left Vietnam on New Year's Eve and headed for Minot, but the two didn't meet until April. Bob drove to Bismarck and met Marlys for coffee. Marlys didn't like coffee, but she drank it anyway. That night they went bowling and the next morning they attended church with Marlys' family.

Marlys admits she liked Bob right away. They hit it off and Bob's trips to Bismarck were more and more frequent. He put 10,000 miles on his car in the first three months. They were engaged before Marlys graduated from high school. They married that August in Bismarck.

Bob had one more year in the Air Force. When his assignment was complete, Bob and Marlys together entered Salvation Army officers' training in Chicago. Two years later the Bohns were ordained as Salvation Army officers. They served congregations in Kansas, North Dakota, and Minnesota, for several years before settling down. Bob continued his education in airplane mechanics and Marlys studied nursing, and they both served as chaplains to a nursing home.

"I think what attracted us to each other," says Marlys, "is that we were both fairly new to Christ and excited about our faith. We have grown together in our faith, which has had its ups and downs ... we have been able to encourage each other. The years have brought maturity and a deepening of our love which would never have happened without the foundation of our faith. The ministry brings about many trying times, but knowing that we were in it together made all the difference to us. Even in our personal lives, it was that foundation and bond of love that sustained us (through difficult times)."

Today Bob works at the Air National Guard and Marlys is a nurse and hospital chaplain. Their faith is strong and they are glad to have had so many opportunities serving God.

(Details taken from a 6/18/99 Fargo *Forum* newspaper article by Erin Hemme Froslie.)

Epiphany 3
Matthew 4:12-23

A Time To Rest, A Time For Renewal

"Now when Jesus heard that John had been arrested, he withdrew to Galilee. He left Nazareth and made his home in Capernaum by the sea, in the territory of Zebulun and Naphtali, so that what had been spoken through the prophet Isaiah might be fulfilled...." (vv. 12-14)

Stan needed rest, but there was no letting up. His schedule was outrageously full: appointments, meetings, consultations, and routine activities kept him in the office and hospital almost eighteen hours a day. As if this weren't enough, medical crises came up during the night, and several nights a week he would be called in to attend to these problems. He missed his wife and children, who went on a European vacation without him. He was running short on steam, as he said to his colleagues. Even though doctors have hectic schedules, he knew he needed a break.

The break came in the form of the flu. It wasn't a welcome break, but it was a break. Stan had worked through lunches, barely taken time to relax, much less get adequate rest at night. And he got sick. Stan coughed and sneezed and ached for three days. His secretary canceled all his appointments and wouldn't give him his messages. Nothing was as urgent as getting well, she said.

So Stan rested. And rested and rested. And he thought and thought and thought.

Stan slept for two days straight and on the third day he took turns between laying in the hammock and on the recliner. He propped open the patio door on the deck so he could feel the ocean breeze. He was starting to feel alive again. He took a week of afternoons off to think, rest, and consider his direction in life.

Stan looked back on the last few weeks and months, the hectic schedule and the extreme hours. It was outrageous. It was unnecessary. He needed to change something. But what?

He prayed and meditated on what the "what" could be all week. His answer came with the visit of his friend, Bill. His friend, also a medical doctor, wanted a change. He wanted to start an urgent care clinic where there would be set hours, set schedules, and a set routine. Bill wanted more time with his wife and children. He wanted time to read medical journals and novels. He wanted to play golf and go the movies a few times a year. He wanted just a little more routine so he could be with his children. Bill was fed up with his present schedule. The words echoed in Stan's ears. It was as if he were hearing his own thoughts of the past week aloud.

Stan and Bill talked long into the night. They talked the next day, Saturday. They dreamed, they schemed, and they thought. They talked to trusted friends, their wives, their children, and most importantly, they prayed about it both together and privately. Was this what God wanted for them?

Eleven months later, plans were made. Bill and Stan were going to open an urgent care center in an old office building. They would renovate the building and make it a welcome place where people could be seen right away. It was a big gamble, but it was worth taking. Doctors were lined up. Equipment had to be ordered, contractors set up and started, and publicity had to begin. It was an enormous task, but one that Stan welcomed. It was as if there were a renewal in his vocation, his passion for helping people.

The urgent care center opened and business was slow for the first month. It gave Stan and Bill a chance to work out more details. Slowly things took off and business was great. But the best thing for Stan was a set schedule, time for his wife and family, and the chance to feel human again. He was renewed, energized to go on with the next fifty years of his life!

Epiphany 4
Micah 6:1-8

An Open Letter To Congressional Delegation And The U.S. Secretary Of Agriculture

"And what does the Lord require of you but to do justice, and to love kindness, and to walk humbly with your God?" (v. 8)

Dear Sirs:

American farmers take their vocations seriously. Not only does farming provide honorable work in a setting conducive to creating a high quality of life — particularly for raising a family — but the farmer's work raises food for a hungry world, and increasingly farm products are also being used as renewable fuel and other innovative non-food products. All of these contribute to both the nation's standard of living and its sustainability.

As believers in the one true God, we also take seriously the requirements listed in Micah 6:8. To farmers, a fair return on their invested labor and resources is all that's expected. The United States government has failed to "do justice" to the American farmer in this respect. Disasters of many kinds — in addition to low prices and poor farm policy — have only exacerbated this problem. Our rural people and communities are suffering greatly from the long- and short-term effects of these problems and they need relief now!

Gentlemen, we appeal to you to take action immediately and declare an agricultural emergency in order to set in motion that which will help begin the rebuilding of our nation's rural and small-town economic and community base, a base that is essential to our country's (and for that matter, the world's) stability and sustainability in the present and in the future.

Respectfully signed,
 A farm family

Sweet/Salty Love

" 'If salt has lost its taste, how can its saltiness be re-
stored? It is no longer good for anything, but is thrown
out and trampled under foot. You are the light of the
world ... let your light shine before others, so that they
may see your good works and give glory to your Father
in heaven.' " (vv. 13-14, 16)

While waiting at the beauty salon, I was captivated by an article in *People* magazine (January 11, 1999). It showed a couple
sporting the same bald hairdo, cuddling up together. The title
pushed me to read further: "Winning at Home: When his wife got
cancer, NFL linebacker Chris Spielman quit the game to help." I
was intrigued.

At the time, Chris Spielman was a linebacker for the National
Football League Buffalo Bills. When his wife Stephanie, who was
recovering from breast cancer, needed him, he quit the team to be
at her side.

Football had been Chris' life for 26 of his 33 years. His father
was a football coach. He grew up in an Ohio town a stone's throw
from Canton, home of the NFL Hall of Fame. He was in the shadow
of football, and it became his life. In high school and college, he
was a football star. As a professional, Chris was a four-time All
Pro, one of the NFL's fiercest competitors who practiced and practiced. He was known to have slept nude with the air conditioner on
to prepare for the brutal winter weather in Buffalo's Rich Stadium.
He was at the top of his game.

But Stephanie was not at the top of her game. She had a growth
on her breast, and during the surgery to remove it, doctors found a
malignant tumor. The entire breast and 28 lymph nodes had to be
removed. It was quite a blow to this former model who became a
full-time mother when her children, Madison and Noah, were born.

When Stephanie's chemotherapy treatments began, Chris' football career was put on hold. He felt it more important to be with his one true passion: his wife. Football was important, but it was secondary to what was occurring. He wanted to support Stephanie not just in words, but in actions. So Chris was in charge of holding Stephanie's hand during her treatments, running the household, and ferrying the children to where they needed to be.

It was a whole different kind of ball game for Chris. He found that the same intensity that drove him to be a successful football player was what helped him focus on learning all he could about cancer and vitamins. The tremendous amount of patience he needed during practice was the same patience he needed for the children. And his passion for life was still the same.

Chris hoped to return to the Buffalo Bills. But while Stephanie needed him, he wanted to be there for her first. Chris had known the sweetness of the game as linebacker. He had known the sweetness of his love for Stephanie and their two children. He had also known the salty taste of cancer and recovery.

The haircuts Chris and Stephanie sported? Chris kept his hair shaved to show solidarity with Stephanie while she was undergoing chemotherapy. Hair could always grow back; precious moments couldn't. Chris had tasted the salt; now he recognized the sweet.

The Stolen Generation

" 'So when you are offering your gift at the altar, if you remember that your brother or sister has something against you, leave your gift there before the altar and go; first be reconciled to your brother or sister, and then come and offer your gift.' " (vv. 23-24)

In an October 2, 2000, *Time* magazine article written by Terry McCarthy, Archie Roach recounts a personal event that changed his private and public world. In fact, the event changed the Aboriginal world forever. A native of Australia, Roach shares the painful moment when welfare officers came to take him to an orphanage because he was not white. Archie is an Aborigine whose grandfather was white.

They came to the house on the premise that they were taking three-year-old Archie to a picnic, but his family knew better. Archie tells of his aunt trying to scare off the welfare officers, but the gun was not loaded and they called her bluff. Thus, Archie was taken from his tin-lined house in Framlingham in southeastern Australia to Melbourne, where the goal was to "assimilate him" at a mission school. They tried to make him more white by forcing his naturally curly hair straight with combs, all to no avail. Archie's hair was curly, and Archie's skin was black. His captors, in a sense, had failed. They told him his family died in a fire. Archie's identity, heritage, and culture were stolen from him.

The Australian government during the early 1900s was trying to bring the mixed-blood Aborigines into the white world in hopes the blackness would be "bred out" in a few generations. The fully black population, on the other hand, was expected to die out. An estimated 100,000 children were stolen in this manner until the practice stopped in 1971.

Now, many years later, the Aboriginal, black, and white sectors of Australia want healing, if that is possible. They have marched across Sydney in numbers swelling to 200,000. They have demonstrated, begged, and debated for an apology.

So far, no apology has been issued. But there is hope. Many thousands have embraced Aborigine athletes. Their plight is being brought to the forefront and whites are willing to admit, apologize, and go on with their lives. They want to live in harmony, but they want to set the record straight and make amends.

There is hope for Australia.

Conscience-Building

"According to the grace of God given to me, like a skilled master builder I laid a foundation, and someone else is building on it. Each builder must choose with care how to build on it. For no one can lay any foundation other than the one that has been laid; that foundation is Jesus Christ." (vv. 10-11)

Trace was known for his strong, durable buildings. They weren't anything spectacular to look at, no works of art, but they were solid. He built barns, machine sheds, and quonsets. Big, burly buildings to hold big, burly machinery and equipment were his specialty, and he stood behind his buildings. He had learned from his grandfather and father and had shown an exceptional eye for detail and was an expert craftsman. Trace was respected for his work, and he never lacked for projects.

Just 27 years old, Trace had had a good life — until his wife of six months ran off with a neighbor. They had no children and Trace felt himself becoming lonelier and lonelier. He would come in from a long day of working, sometimes out in the cold and wind, and he had no one to turn to for companionship, love, or conversation. He eventually turned to alcohol for comfort.

Trace went on drinking binges, often falling asleep on the couch in front of a blaring television set. He ate poorly and his judgment started to fall short. He felt like he was falling into a pit of darkness. He was working on a big machine shed for a wealthy farmer and Trace found that he wasn't measuring as accurately, his orders didn't match what he needed, and the work was not going as effortlessly as it normally had in the past. He knew he had to do something.

His wife had certainly left him, but Trace had many friends in his hometown. They begged him to take care of himself, to get a hold of himself, to turn around from the brink of despair. All their pleading worked and slowly Trace started to come out of his depression. He spent more time with his friends and family. He took better care of his orders, his work was more accurate, and his judgment was once again keen.

About a month later, the farmer called him to say his sliding barn door didn't work quite right. The door was on the working end of the huge machine shed Trace put up right when he was in the middle of his sadness, right when his perception was blurred, right when things were not going quite right for Trace. Trace drove out to the farm to speak with the owner, who complained of a door that was sticking on the way up.

Trace looked at the shed. It was crooked. His trained eye could see that although it was only a fraction of an inch off, it was definitely crooked. The wall was not straight and the door, which was pulled up by heavy chains, was getting caught by the crooked wall. To an untrained person, the shed looked fine: it was big and square, and the walls were very high. But Trace was an expert, and when he examined the shed closely, he knew he had done a poor job. The farmer didn't guess that, but Trace could see it as plain as day.

There was no way Trace could afford new materials. Yet he knew he had not done the best he could do. He was in a quandary. The farmer thought the door needed oil; Trace knew it was much, much more.

Trace told the farmer, an old family friend, not to use the door and that he would be back in a few days to fix it. It wasn't spring yet and the farmer wouldn't need to move machinery for several weeks. Trace would be back.

What Trace really needed to do was think about the situation. He had paid over $130,000 for materials for the shed and had gained twice that much in labor. But that money was already spent on the double quonset he was building at the west end of town for the city works department. He knew it would be easy to bend the wall a bit and ease the door framing so the door could pass easier, but it would never hold over the years. And the mechanism had to be just right

43

to work well or the door could get stuck or even worse, fall. The farmer needed to move machinery in and out of the shed often during the spring planting season and the fall harvest time. He could be in danger if the door didn't work right. Trace knew he needed to rebuild, but he didn't know how to tell the farmer, or how he would pay for some additional materials he would need.

Trace wasn't big on going to church, but he loved the small town's only pastor. Pastor Eldred was an older man who had been there 32 years and had seen Trace grow up. He had been the one to marry Trace and Janet last summer. Pastor Eldred had been there when the family experienced the trauma of death and illness, and he had been there to see the joys of births, baptisms, and weddings. Trace had always regarded Pastor Eldred to be the family's pastor, not his personal pastor. But right now Trace needed the older man's wisdom. Maybe if he could debate aloud, he could get a handle on what to do. Trace called and would see Pastor Eldred that evening after supper.

Trace and Pastor Eldred exchanged pleasantries for a while, and the pastor asked about each family member by name. Then Pastor Eldred smiled and looked Trace squarely in the eyes. "What's on your mind, Trace? How can I help you be the person you would like to be?"

Wow! Trace wasn't expecting that kind of question. He sincerely didn't know what to say, and so he looked down at his feet, noticing his shoelace was untied. He bent down to tie it. He looked around the room and noticed the picture frame askew about a sixteenth of an inch. He'd have to fix that after Pastor Eldred left.

Pastor Eldred smiled again. "Trace, what's troubling you? I'm so sorry about Janet. I imagine you are quite lonely at times, but what is really troubling your heart right now?"

Trace stood up. He was quite nervous. He had wanted to debate with Pastor Eldred on what to do about the shed, but he knew he couldn't pull the wool over his eyes. He sat down again and blurted out the situation, telling Pastor Eldred about the building he had put up. It was a poor job, not like he would normally do, and he didn't know what to do about it.

"Yes, you do, Trace. I know your reputation for exactness. You have always stood behind your work, just like your grandpa and daddy taught you. You know what to do. You just have to have the courage to explain the truth to the farmer. You don't need me to tell you that. I just need to remind you that you need to be true to yourself. Be the person you really are, the best you can be. And I need to remind you that God loves you — with or without Janet — happy or sad, through thick and thin. You can make this right or you can take the easy way out. Just consider your future with either option. Fix it and you will be out lots of money, but you will also be a hero for being honest. Ignore it and you could put someone in danger, and who will come to you for work? You know what to do and I will leave you to get on with it and do your best. Say hi to your parents for me."

Trace felt like a five-year-old as he watched his dear friend leave. He knew what to do, and although he'd be out thousands of dollars, he knew the right thing would be to tear down the shed and start over, being more exact this time. He knew what God wanted him to do.

He picked up the phone to call the farmer.

Today's Trouble Is Enough For Today

---

*" 'So do not worry about tomorrow, for tomorrow will
bring worries of its own. Today's trouble is enough for
today.' " (v. 34)*

Margy was born in 1934. It was a difficult year: the family was
struggling to keep the farm, and wheat prices were very low. The
cattle were dying, and optimism was a distant memory.

Margy's sister was born four years later. Margy remembers
watching her mother's tummy grow, and Margy's excitement about
the birth of the baby grew along with it. Finally the time grew near.
A woman came to help, and Margy's father looked pale. Margy
remembers her mother asking if Margy could sleep over with a
playmate. Margy took her dolly and her pajamas. She and her friend
played baby long into the night.

Two days later, Margy's father came to pick her up. He looked
sad, and Margy was confused. She didn't say a word. Her father
didn't say a word. He just looked sad. Her mother met them at the
door. She hugged Margy tightly and told her that a baby girl had
been born to them but had only lived a few minutes and that she
wasn't there anymore. Margy didn't understand, but the sounds of
her mother's sobs told her that something had gone terribly wrong.

Margy wondered about her baby sister. She missed her even as
her mother had another baby girl and two little boys later on. Margy
accepted it as one of life's mysteries — until she was married and
ready to have children of her own. She finally broached the un-
speakable subject. What happened to her baby sister?

Her mother couldn't answer. Twenty-five years later, it was
still too painful. Margy asked her father: the baby's cord came first
and as the neighbor woman tugged, the baby turned blue. They

weren't sure what to do, and they held the baby and watched as her final breath was taken from her.

Her father cried when he shared the story. He said after all those years, he still thought of that perfect little baby, so still, so quiet. He hadn't known what to do at the time. His wife was despondent, so he had a private funeral by the pond for the baby. The baby was wrapped in the best quilt, and Margy's father had taken the time to make a casket from lumber scraps. He cried and said prayers for the baby.

Times certainly had changed, he told Margy. In those days, the birth of a child was looked at with fear. Women commonly wondered if they would live through the event. Many babies died in the process. He hugged Margy tightly and assured her that today this wouldn't happen. Nurses would be on hand. She would be just fine.

Margy and her husband had two healthy children in four years with no trouble with either birth. She told her children when they were old enough to understand what happened to their aunt. Margy's parents never spoke about her sister again, but Margy felt her little sister's life — ever so brief — should still be honored. After Margy's parents died, Margy had three memorial markers made: one for her father, one for her mother, and one for her baby sister.

Transfiguration Of Our Lord
2 Peter 1:16-21

A Defining Moment

"First of all you must understand this, that no prophecy of scripture is a matter of one's own interpretation, because no prophecy ever came by human will, but men and women moved by the Holy Spirit spoken from God."
(v. 21)

Sue went with her three most trusted friends on a retreat. "Pray for me as I will pray for each of you," she said. "Pray that I will make the right decision for my future."

Rachel, who wanted to go to spend time reflecting on the Psalms, had invited Sue to the priory. Rachel had also invited Amy, who was dealing with destructive family issues. Amy wanted Debbie to come because her faith had been renewed, and they wanted to share in her exuberance. The foursome made plans.

Sue, Debbie, Rachel, and Amy regularly prayed together and alone at Bible study, during coffee time, and at church. They prayed for each other and with each other: they were very close friends. They made a commitment to be with each other for a weekend so that they could be closer to God in an environment with minimal distraction: a priory. They knew in their everyday lives they could draw close to God at any time in prayer or meditation, but they were intentional about their efforts to be free from interruption and responsibility for just these 72 hours.

Seventy-two hours. Time to breathe deeply, walk in the woods, sit on the dock, or lie in a hammock. Seventy-two hours to focus on one area of their lives and ask God to guide them. They would spend the time in silence to listen to God's words, to listen to the sounds around them, and to listen to what their hearts were needing.

Sue came to the priory with an agenda. She had a deadline. She had had a secret wish to become a pastor for over twenty years, but she had four children, and had taken care of them at home and focused all her attention on them until they were young adults. As they grew, so did her yearning for ministry. She and her husband helped out at the church whenever and wherever they could, even stepping in while the pastor was on vacation. Sue loved church life, but — at the age of 46 — what could she do about it?

There was an urgency now: Sam, her friend, was the chaplain at a seminary and he invited Sue and her husband over. Sam told them he wanted Sue to come for Seminary Days, and he would be with her at all the events. Sam knew Sue loved the church and enjoyed helping out, but Sue wondered if he knew more than he let on. Sue had told her husband of her dream only a few years ago, when their youngest graduated from high school. But Sam was persistent, promising them afternoon trips to the nearby ocean if they would come. Sue promised Sam she would let him know. Next week she had to make up her mind.

What should she do? Her husband, Carl, was so well suited at his job as manager at a manufacturing plant. He enjoyed being with the workers. He had a reputation of being tough yet very fair in his dealings with other companies. He worked hard but was able to be home on weekends. They knew his generous income had afforded them the luxury that allowed Sue to stay home with the children. To leave that life would be a great risk. To reestablish somewhere else in a new profession would be an even greater risk. Was it worth it?

Their lifestyle allowed them time to donate money and give many hours to charities. They liked their freedom to travel and wanted to help the children become independent. But now it was Sue's turn. What would she do? What should she do? What did God want her to do? She hoped to find some direction on her long weekend.

At the priory, the four hugged and smiled often, but they were not allowed to speak to one another. It added another dimension to their friendship. The usual conversations, debates, joking and sup-porting of one another was absent in the silence. Yet they knew they were holding each other up in prayer. And prayer is what gave Sue strength.

Praying for guidance and a heart that would be still, ready to listen, Sue asked God to come close to her. She wanted to listen; she wanted guidance. She just wanted to know what God wanted her to do for the future. She was sitting quietly at the end of the dock, kicking her feet in the water, when suddenly she was overcome with emotion. It began as a small cry, then a few tears followed by a steady flow of tears. Sue wasn't sure what she was crying about, but she knew she wasn't sad. Her tears were a sort of cleansing. She prayed that God would help interpret her tears, her emotions, her thoughts. She continued to cry quietly at the end of the dock as the leaves rustled in the trees nearby.

The water was very calm. Sue looked into the water and saw the face of her dear Carl, who was very supportive of her. He had told her he would give up his job and find something else if she wanted to pursue ministry. It would be her choice.

She saw the face of her children, now well on their way to becoming established adults, secure in their careers. She saw the faces of Debbie, Rachel, and Amy, who were there through thick and thin. They had sat with her when her mother was dying of cancer; they waited with her through soccer tryouts and recital rehearsals. She felt so fortunate, so grateful for them.

A comforting presence was all around her, and Sue felt very peaceful as she sat on that dock. It was as if she were reliving important moments of her life as she remembered her childhood, her marriage, events with her husband, and times with her children. Things that happened at church, at her children's schools, and at her husband's work came racing across her mind, in short spurts. Flashes of memories flooded her mind and she felt an overwhelming feeling of gratitude.

Sue started saying a prayer of thanks for the many, many blessings she had. She was so grateful for her life, for her husband, for her children. Her friends, her church and her community fitted her well.

The tears stopped and Sue felt both drained but hopeful. She felt exactly as she did after a five-mile run: tired yet somehow very energized. She splashed the water with her feet as she leaned against the dock post. She didn't have an answer yet, but she knew she was somehow changed. She closed her eyes and concentrated on the sun shining on her face. She had confidence she would know what to do very soon. God was with her; she could feel it. And God would guide her.

A Random Act Of Kindness

---

*" 'Beware of practicing your piety before others in or-
der to be seen by them; for then you have no reward
from your Father in heaven ... For where your treasure
is, there your heart will be also.' " (vv. 1, 20)*

In his book *A Time to Fish and A Time to Dry Nets* (1996:
Lakewood Publishing Co.), author Alvin Johnston tells about his
roots in Warroad, Minnesota. His grandfather, Grandpa Gruhl, arrived in Warroad in 1896 with his wife Sofia and their five children, having traveled in two covered wagons. Sofia and her newborn baby were in the wagon while the children walked behind.
Sofia and baby Anna Belle died of consumption (tuberculosis) the
first winter they were in Warroad.

Johnston's mother, Mabel, was the second of these five children. In Johnston's book, Mabel recalls how difficult, boring, and
long the days were in a one-room house. Their father would be
gone days at a time hunting or working in the woods. Mabel, who
was twelve, served as housekeeper for her family. It was a difficult
situation to be in. It seems others were noticing her situation also.

Mabel remembers one day when she and her sister heard foot-
steps outside the door. Thinking it was their father, they rushed to
open the door only to find an old American Indian man standing
there. "His forehead was covered with scar tissue and he was bald-
headed. Taking one look at him, the girls crawled under a bed, so
frightened they could not move. They knew he came as a friend
when he held out a fresh piece of moose meat. Their visitor, called
Ayashwas, was the chief of Warroad and Buffalo Point tribes. A
kindly old man, he had stopped by their cabin to help them out. He
was a great warrior in the fierce battle between his people and the

Sioux. On a ridge called Two Rivers, over fifty years before, he was scalped and left for dead on the battlefield."

Winters were very difficult with the harsh weather and an entire family crowded into one room. States Johnston, "... the kindness of the local Indians saved them by bringing them venison, rabbits, and moose meat. That winter a bond was formed between the local Indians and our family that lasted through three generations."

Beware of practicing your piety before others in order to be seen by them, for then you have no reward from your Father in heaven ... For where your treasure is, there your heart will be also.

Lent 1
Romans 5:12-19

Rainbow

"But the free gift is not like the trespass. For if the many died through the one man's trespass, much more surely have the grace of God and the free gift in the grace of the one man, Jesus Christ, abounded for the many." (v. 15)

The clown came walking ever so slowly up the aisle, smiling. She looked around. She was holding a picnic basket. Her face was white, her hair was red, her suit was brightly striped, and her pointed hat was a shiny blue. Her mouth was painted, but it neither smiled nor frowned. It was a wondering kind of expression.

Rainbow walked up the aisle, up the steps, up toward the altar. She took a quick look at the congregation and slowly shrugged her shoulders. It was an exaggerated shrug with shoulders raised and held high. All was very quiet. She looked up at the enormous cross suspended above the altar. She walked backwards, away from the altar, until she was at the edge of the steps. She set her picnic basket down. From behind the altar she took a small table and put it by the basket — dead center on the ground in front of the altar. She took out a brightly colored feather duster and carefully, slowly, meticulously, stroked the table's surface. Clean! She turned to us and smiled.

Quietly and slowly, she opened her picnic basket and took out a bright red checkered table cloth. Rainbow shook it out and ever so carefully placed it on the small table. She took out two star-shaped crystal candle holders. She put them to her eyes and got a few laughs. She hid her face. All was quiet again in the large sanctuary.

Gently, she put the candle holders on the table, one at each end. Gingerly, she placed two red candles in them, assessing their placement all the while. She moved them an inch to the left, then a half inch to the right, then toward the middle a bit. Satisfied, she reached for some matches and tried to light them. They wouldn't light. Rainbow looked around and quietly walked through the congregation. She handed the matches to a gentleman, who quietly followed her and lit her candles. She smiled broadly and gave him a big hug. His cheeks seemed a shade brighter as he made his way back to the pew.

Rainbow went back to the basket. She put a ceramic urn at the back of the little table. It was about the size of her palm. She reached for a cross made of two twigs. Rainbow stepped back, looked up and considered the huge cross suspended above her, above the altar. She looked at the twigs. She held them up. She straightened the arms of the cross. She put the twigs in the urn. She looked up at the cross and smiled.

From the basket she took out a circle of vines. Her hand snapped back as she reached for it. Her face twisted in pain. She picked it up, only much more carefully and slowly. She lifted up the circle and looked at it. She looked around and shyly put the circle on her head. She winced in pain. She looked at it again, and her face was overcome with sadness. She looked up at the cross again. Her shoulders seemed to slump forward as she put the circle around the cross.

Rainbow took a step back and eyed the table. She looked around and then at the basket. From it she took a plate and put it in the center of the table. Then she lifted out a loaf of bread and a cloth. She put the bread on the plate and covered it with the cloth. Suddenly, she yanked the cloth off and looked at the loaf. She wrapped the bread in the cloth and held it like a baby in the crook of her arm. She bent down to give it a kiss. She cradled it and hugged it tightly. Gently, she set it on the plate and placed the cloth on top. The cloth seemed to caress the body of bread.

She stepped back, looked again at the cross on the altar. She paused, then reached for the twig cross in the small urn. She held the twig cross up but the circle started to slide. She lifted the cross again and the circle slid the other way. She grabbed the circle, but her hand sprang back quickly. Her mouth was twisted and her eyes were closed. She opened them again and held up the cross and the

55

circle all at once. She picked up the bread and slid it in front of the cross, under the circle.

Rainbow stopped. She stuck out her lower lip as she looked away at the huge cross suspended above the altar. Her body twisted and she grasped the loaf of bread and tore it in half. Her eyes grew bigger and her mouth opened. Rainbow quickly put the bread halves on the plate and the cross back in the urn. The only sound in the church was the swish of Rainbow's shiny, striped coveralls.

Rainbow reached for a bottle from the basket. She lifted it up, then set it down on the table. She looked at the twig cross in the urn and pulled it from the urn. She rotated the cross on its side. She put the bottle at the end of the turned-down arm and held it there. Her body bent over a little also, as if the blood were draining out of her arm. Not a sound was heard.

She bent down to reach for a goblet and poured into it from the bottle. She lifted the goblet up and held it there for all to see. All 1,200 of us. She looked at us and smiled.

She put her basket behind the altar and reached for a box, wrapped in shiny white paper with a big bow on top. Rainbow lifted the lid and peered inside. She looked at the congregation and smiled a slow, big smile. She took out a sign that said, "For You." She placed it in front of the table, stepped back and looked at the table. She smiled at the congregation, picked up her picnic basket, and slowly walked out of the church. We were silent.

This was the beginning of Lent. The choir had sung a beautiful hymn, the lessons had been read, and the pastor moved us with a powerful sermon. We were ready to acknowledge our sinfulness and begin the passion journey. But we couldn't be ready until we received a gift at the altar, under the cross. Rainbow had interpreted for us the greatest gift of all: that of the blood and body of God's only son, Jesus, who died on the cross.

Poor Nicodemus
(or ... "Some People Just Don't Get It")

"Jesus answered him, 'Very truly I tell you, no one can see the kingdom of God without being born from above.'" (v. 3)

Nicodemus didn't get it. He heard Jesus' words, but it doesn't seem that he understood what Jesus was saying. Nicodemus was a Pharisee, a ruler in the Jewish world. He was one of the more liberal Pharisees because he even considered having a debate with Jesus. He respectfully called Jesus "Rabbi." Rabbis taught that the keeping of the law would allow the kingdom of God to come, but Jesus turned the conversation around and said that indeed salvation in the kingdom of God requires a new way of thinking, a rebirth, so to speak.

Bob experienced a rebirth at the ripe age of 32. He wasn't a bad person; he just was not into "faith." An accountant by profession, Bob liked his world to be neat. His office was simple but furnished with furniture of excellent quality. His couch was of Italian leather, his lamp of Austrian crystal, and his art from fine galleries. His mahogany desk was uncluttered, and his reports were meticulous in detail. He liked his world to be orderly.

Bob liked his computer to be a certain way, his regular coffee with just the right amount of creamer in it, and his clothes pressed to perfection. Bob wasn't a flashy dresser, but he bought the best suits he could afford. He just liked the clean look they gave him. The barber trimmed his hair every two-and-a-half weeks and every morning he swam exactly eight laps in the huge pool at the gym. He bought a paper on the way to work before boarding the subway train, and he arrived at exactly seventeen minutes before eight every morning. He was comfortable. He liked things a certain way. His life was orderly.

Then he met Jennie. Jennie worked as a clerk for another accountant down the hall. She brought Bob the morning reports and would swish away as fast as she could. She thought Bob was weird, a little "anal-retentive" as she put it, a bit eccentric. She was also curious about this man with exquisite taste.

Bob never even noticed her at first. He usually took the reports without even looking at her and quickly got to work on the day's assignments. It wasn't that he was particularly unfriendly; he just liked to get to work. He hardly ever took a break, rarely left the office for lunch, and worked until exactly 23 minutes past six in the evening, when he could take a nice walk to the subway station and be home just before seven in the evening. It was a comfortable routine.

Jennie didn't like routine; she thought it was boring. One morning she set the reports down in front of Bob and sat down on his couch. He didn't even notice. She put her feet up on his couch. He glanced up and was surprised to see her there. "Yes?" was all he could say. He wanted to get busy with his reports.

"What a great couch! And that lamp is so beautiful! Look at the way it catches the light. It's casting a rainbow onto the wall over there. See you tomorrow!" With that, she dashed out of the office, her long skirt making a swishing sound.

Bob went back to his work. Then he glanced up to see the rainbow reflecting off the lamp he had bought in Austria last year. It was beautiful. But he had work to do. The next morning Jennie came in with flavored coffee. She wanted Bob to try it. He didn't want to be rude, but he mentioned he already had his coffee. But Jennie was persistent and made him try it. It was almond-flavored. It was delicious. But he had work to do.

Another day Jennie came in just before noon and mentioned she needed to borrow some money for lunch because she forgot her wallet. "Let's grab a bite to eat downstairs in the café across from the park!" She was so excited, so naïve to think Bob would actually stop for lunch. She argued that he had to eat anyway and that she would repay him in the morning. They headed down for the café.

They ate sandwiches and drank colas. Bob hardly said a word at lunch, but he did straighten his napkin across his lap and made sure the glass was clean before pouring his cola. He was thinking of finishing his report to present to their manager. Jennie was going on and on about the beautiful day, and when he unknowingly said, "Uh-huh," to her question, it was too late. She had asked him if he enjoyed the park as much as she did. She laughed at his "uh-huh," stood up, and grabbed his arm. She pulled him to the sidewalk, and there they began their first of many walks.

Bob told Jennie she shouldn't be interested in him: he was boring, loved his work, and never did anything exciting. But Jennie didn't believe it. They talked about her love of music, his love of traveling, and a shared interest in the arts. Their walks became a daily ritual until they were comfortable enough to go out on a date. They were so different in many ways: Jennie's clothes were bought at a discount store, she didn't like to fuss with her unruly mop of curls, and she didn't really care if her slip showed a bit now and then. She had a zest for life that was infectious. Soon Bob felt himself falling in love with her.

Jennie had a faith that was very deep, very emotional, and very personal. She had a hard time explaining to Bob what her faith meant to her. To her it was as if God were all around, in the beautiful fall leaves, the rainbow, and the rain storms. God was in the flowers on her desk, in the piano she played so well, and in the classical music she loved to listen to. Indeed, for her, God was in Bob's beloved paintings.

But Bob didn't get it. The world was either black or white, a yes or a no; it was not emotional, passionate, or feeling. He didn't understand Jennie's faith.

Jennie took Bob with her to church, to her Bible study, and to retreats. Slowly, Bob began to see the world in a not-so-black-and-white world. He could feel the passion of the Psalms, the torment and anger in the exile story, the love Mary had for her baby. Bible stories started to speak to him on an emotional level, and Bob finally starting to "get it." God was in the life of everyone and everything. Faith was available for everyone without regard to following a formula. Faith was something that Bob wanted.

Ten years ago, Bob found God at the age of 32, two years after he met Jennie and one year before they got married. He still likes his life a certain way but he as made concessions: one of which is almond-flavored coffee, taking time for lunch, and not worrying if one of the children messes up his schedule. Bob has a love for God that goes beyond measure. He's learned to let go and let God into his world. Indeed, there is room for faith in Bob's orderly world.

Lent 3
Romans 5:1-11

The Faith Of Rachel Bella Calof

"Therefore, since we are justified by faith, we have peace with God: suffering produces endurance, and endurance produces character, and character produces hope, and hope does not disappoint us, because God's love has been poured into our hearts through the Holy Spirit that has been given to us." (vv. 1, 4-5)

This passage fits the life of Rachel Bella Kahn Calof. The book, *Rachel Calof's Story* (Jacob Calof: Indiana University Press, 1995) tells the story about this remarkable woman who had to endure setbacks and disasters before becoming convinced that God was indeed with her. She never evoked pity from her readers. She plainly detailed the ordeals she had to endure as a young woman brought from Russia to be the wife of a homesteader in North Dakota before the turn of the century.

Rachel's life started out disastrously: her mother died when she was four, her father married a cruel stepmother, and the children had to tolerate beatings before being farmed out to other families by their father. Rachel became a maid at her aunt's house, was not allowed to speak to a boy (a butcher) she had fallen in love with because his position in life was "below hers," and finally was designated to be the mail-order bride for a homesteader across the ocean.

"Shock and deprivation were no strangers in my young life," she wrote, "but seeing what faced us in this new and hostile environment, I could hardly choke back my tears of grief." Her "welcome to America" supper consisted of a rare treat of boiled dough and cheese. A twelve by fourteen foot shanty gave no privacy to the seven people, chickens, and one cow who had to occupy it. Thus her life in America began.

Cow dung served as their fuel. When fuel ran out, icicles built up in their house until daylight would melt them. Every winter, Rachel, her husband Abraham, her children, and various in-laws would make her house their home to save fuel. It was a terrible burden on her, having to follow religious customs, yet still making a home for herself and her family. She fought bouts of deep depressions. "Of all the privation I knew as a homesteader, the lack of privacy was the hardest to bear," she wrote in her memoirs. There was no chance for private discussions or intimacy.

One day was particularly difficult. "I gave myself up to utter despair. As the tears ran down my cheeks, I reflected upon the course of this miserable life. My early childhood passed through my mind, the time of the servant girl and then my cruel stepmother, followed by seven years with my religiously fanatic grandfather. Within memory I could not recall having lived in a house which I could call home. Little tenderness had ever been shown me. I had tried so hard to raise myself to a decent life, but my way seemed ever downward until now my existence was hardly above the level of an animal. Dear God, I thought, whatever your reasons, haven't I suffered enough in my nineteen years to pay for the rest of my life? ... The pioneer life had brought me to the brink of desperation. Yet as always, a spark of resistance to my lot and a core of determination remained within me, and by morning I was prepared to continue toward my goal. Despair gave birth to courage. Thank God! I would have great need of it before long. Time and again my resolve was to be tested to the limit."

Every year, Rachel and Abraham learned a bit more from their previous year's trials, and every year life did somehow get a little easier, until they were able to build a bigger home. Rachel, her husband, and their children were finally able to experience life as a family unit. They were able to follow their religious customs and praise their God in their own tradition. Only after years and years of insurmountable obstacles and intolerable suffering was Rachel able to become her own person: a person of courage, strength, and enduring character. God was finally tangible, finally present in Rachel Bella's life.

Lent 4
Ephesians 5:8-14

That Which Is Good And Right And True

"For once you were darkness, but now in the Lord you are light. Live as children of light — for the fruit of the light is found in all that is good and right and true. Try to find out what is pleasing to the Lord." (vv. 8-10)

Many, many people have tried to give a formula for the secret of happiness. Some give complex rules that have to be followed. Others declare a person is either lucky — or unlucky. Some give up and feebly give the Ten Commandments as the secret to happiness. Still others feel happiness is only attained by being rich, beautiful, or successful. Rarely do people give a list of things to look at in life to focus attention on the blessings one has.

Author Robin Silverman, in her acclaimed book *The Ten Gifts*, gives positive guidelines to bring peace about in a person's life. Her ways are not a complicated list of do's and don'ts; they are natural ways to bring about joy and harmony in a person's life. As a deeply religious person, Robin has found ways to focus on living in the light, as children of light. The fruit of light, then, is found in all that is good and right and true.

Following is a shortened version of her ten gifts:

1) The Gift Of Warning: Learn to listen to your common sense and your inner promptings. When something makes you fearful, get quiet and ask yourself, "What's better than this?" Follow the directions of your still, small voice within.

2) The Gift Of Refuge: When you're feeling joyless, find a place of refuge. This can be a physical place, or taking refuge in prayer,

music, reading, and so on. Discover new joy by focusing on what is close to you in the present moment.

3) The Gift Of Love: Be fearless about asking for the help you want or need. Accept the good that others offer you, and be willing to respond unconditionally with your best.

4) The Gift Of Surrender: If life seems to be going against you, let go. Stop insisting that things have to be a certain way, and open to the wonder and awe of how wonderful they can be.

5) The Gift Of Simplicity: Eliminate, eliminate, eliminate. Get rid of clutter. Eat simpler foods. Plan fewer activities each day. Delegate. Give away everything you no longer need that you spend your time defending, insuring, maintaining, or managing.

6) The Gift Of Action: Begin anything that feels right to you. Make it a baby step, rather than a giant one, so you won't put off doing it. Just start.

7) The Gift Of Return: Instead of always worrying about what others think of you, get comfortable with who you are right now. Welcome yourself home. Do the same for others.

8) The Gift Of Commitment: Decide where and how you're going to spend your energy. Ask yourself: "Who do I want to BE?" Be that. Keep making the same choice over and over, no matter what others say. Commit to your values, your abilities, your nature, and your ideas.

9) The Gift Of Trust: Begin treating all of your relationships and encounters as holy. Assume that each one is meant as a gift or an opportunity for you to show your own light to the world.

10) The Gift Of Thanks: Count your blessings. Pray. Find the good around you and praise it.

"For once you were darkness, but now in the Lord you are light. Live as children of light — for the fruit of the light is found in all that is good and right and true. Try to find out what is pleasing to the Lord."

For more information, write to:
Robin Silverman
Creativisions
P. O. Box 13135
Grand Forks, ND 58208-3135

Funerals

"The Jews who were with her in the house, her...."
(v. 31)

Cheryl's father had an affair with his secretary when Cheryl was just four years old. Cheryl's mother, who had battled several bouts of depression, was overcome with grief and committed suicide. This left Cheryl, her two older brothers, and three sisters in the care of their father and his girlfriend.

The funeral was a somber affair: people were in shock at what happened and saddened to see the children left behind. There was also angry talk about the scandalous affair that was now public. People stared at the children and gossip abounded. Cheryl doesn't remember much about it except that her father's girlfriend sat at the very back of the church all alone. She thought that was strange because the children knew she was moving into their home that night.

Cheryl, her brothers, and sisters, all grew up, and though they didn't really like their stepmother very well, their lives were basically uneventful. No one had trouble with the law or drugs or had unwanted children. They simply grew up, secured good jobs, and moved away. Their family wasn't very close; however, they did come together when there was a need.

When Cheryl turned 34, her stepmother — now 52 — developed breast cancer. After a radical mastectomy and the removal of several lymph nodes, the prognosis was not good: the cancer had metastasized and spread into the chest area. They had caught it very, very late. The warning signs had been ignored and there was not much the doctors could do. She was near death.

Selfish and egocentric were not words to describe Cheryl, yet she felt tremendous guilt over not wanting to visit her father and stepmother, who lived only three hours away. Cheryl normally had minimal contact with her father. She didn't harbor anger at him, but she didn't really approve of his past behavior either. She didn't have much to do with him.

Cheryl's stepmother died within a week of her mastectomy. Cheryl decided she would go to the funeral and pay her respects. It was scheduled for Saturday. She would come to the worship service alone, hug her father, and leave immediately.

But that's not how funerals go. One brother called and then a sister called. Could they all get together a little earlier to help their father set up food? What if they each brought something to take the burden off the father? There was no church involved, no women's group to help. It was up to the children. Cheryl didn't want to be involved, but she begrudgingly came early that Friday with two huge salads in tow. Her husband would pick up their ten-year-old twin boys after school and come to spend the night.

Slowly, the preparation time turned into a reunion of sorts. All the children were there. They talked about their mother's funeral and filled Cheryl in since she had been so young. A brother just a little older than Cheryl shared how angry he was that his mother had shot herself. A sister shared that she hated the stepmother but was afraid that if she showed that hate, the stepmother might also shoot herself. There was much hurt in that home as the children remembered their past. But there was also much healing taking place. Nothing miraculous occurred. There was no flash of light, no lifting of hatred or resentment. But there was a strong sense of forgiveness as the children discussed what it would be like to live with a woman with untreated depression.

They tried not to make excuses for their father's actions, but the brothers wondered if their father had reached the end of his rope when he reached out for his secretary. Could they understand a little better what had happened now that they were grown with families of their own?

Their father joined them that evening and saw all the preparations. He was amazed and grateful. He told them he would have understood if none of them had come. Instead all six of his children were present. He shared how he met the children's mother, a beautiful woman who had wanted to be a singer. Her voice, although pretty, was not exceptional, and she couldn't bear the rejection when she didn't get singing parts in plays. She had become more despondent after the difficult births of each child, and only in hindsight did he see that she should have had medical intervention.

Cheryl's father choked back tears when he shared how freeing it was to tell his secretary that his wife was not well. They didn't mean for anything to happen, but the father needed to talk, and the secretary was willing to listen. After weeks and weeks of talking and sharing their feelings, they had let their feelings become intimate.

He made no excuses for himself. He turned to his children and admitted that what he did was wrong, although in a way he never regretted the chance to unburden himself. He stood there with his head hung low and told them he didn't expect forgiveness, just a little understanding.

The children were riveted. They had never heard so many words come from their father, much less personal words about the past, their mother, and their stepmother. Their father went upstairs to go to sleep, but the children talked through the night, questioning, debating, rebutting.

It was a good night. A good night to air their feelings, understand what the others felt, and clear misunderstandings. Cheryl says now that although she hadn't wanted to go to the funeral, it was the best thing that ever happened to her family. It gave them a chance to be supportive of their father, find understanding, and to be with each other. Each sibling had to come to his or her own terms with the past, but Cheryl feels a huge sense of relief to hear her father's side and to know her stepmother was emphatic about her love for her father. She feels that with time there is hope for reconciliation for all involved. They can never be the Ozzie and Harriet type of family, but they can become more of a family. Thanks to shared feelings, spoken words, and a funeral.

Sorry!

"Judas, his betrayer, repented and brought back the thirty pieces of silver to the chief priests and the elders. 'I have sinned by betraying innocent blood.' But they said, 'What is that to us? See to it yourself.' Throwing down the pieces of silver in the temple, he departed; and he went and hanged himself." (vv. 3-5)

What if Judas hadn't betrayed Jesus? What if Judas wasn't sorry? What if Judas had been a good man and could resist the temptation of money?

I asked my confirmation teacher this and he just stared at me. I think he was a little surprised that I even wondered, or perhaps he thought I was being facetious. He told us that someone had to betray Jesus or the truth from Scripture wouldn't be fulfilled. I had to think about that.

Judas had to betray Jesus; Judas had to be a traitor. We don't. But we find ourselves hardly being able to resist the temptations around us: food, money, possessions. What if we yield to these temptations and are later sorry? That's what happened to two boys, Chato and Gordito Gringo.

Chato, meaning "flat nose," was a tall boy with a pock-marked face. He wore a red bandana so low one could hardly see the slits of his half-closed eyes. He was part of a gang, and he was known for his cruel antics during a new gang member's initiation. He was responsible for an amputated thumb, an eye that was poked out, and numerous burns on limbs. He vehemently denies that one boy is sterile due to electrical burns. Chato was not afraid to administer electric shock or give cigarette burns or cuts to these young boys during his initiations. His victims were those who professed they wanted to be a part of the gang. He intended to have them prove they could stand up to the leaders and "take the heat." Chato was mean.

Gordito Gringo, which means "fat white boy," was also tall. He was also very heavy. Weighing in at almost 300 pounds, he wanted to be a part of the gang. The trouble was that he wasn't very agile, he wasn't very clever, and he wasn't very fast. But he was Chato's best friend, and he wanted the prestige of riding in a low-rider car with girls at his disposal. He wanted to be cool. He and Chato had grown up in side-by-side duplexes; they had known each other their whole lives. Chato had seen Gordito's father die in gang crossfire. Gordito had seen Chato's mother beaten half to death by a jealous boyfriend. They knew the others' sisters intimately and there was hardly anything they wouldn't do for each other. They were inseparable, and Gordito wanted to be in Chato's gang.

Chato wanted Gordito to be in the gang too, but he had to convince the hierarchy. The "hierarchy" consisted of three seventeen-year-olds who led the gang. They determined when there would be a rumble with the neighboring gang. They determined when there would be a drive-by shooting. And they determined who could be in their esteemed organization. They had a proliferation of girl-friends, all "tested" for purity and willing to be devoted to their leaders. Venereal disease was rampant and pregnancy was commonplace. Chato, being the lead initiator, had access to the girls, drugs, and weapons.

So it came time for Chato to initiate Gordito. It was a chilly night. Chato made Gordito drink gasoline, eat dog feces, and ride around naked on the back of a truck. Gordito was encouraged because Chato had promised him he'd go easy on him. Still Chato had to show Gordito was a "man." He put an electrical wire up Gordito's nose and zapped it. Gordito didn't seem to notice. Chato upped the voltage and put the wire on Gordito's chest. He pushed the button. Gordito had a strange look on his face and fell forward. Chato's eyes grew wide and he laughed. Gordito — what a cut up! He had almost convinced Chato that he was dead or something. What a guy! Chato would have to up the voltage. He kicked Gordito, causing him to roll over.

Gordito didn't look right. His eyes were open and the brown parts were looking upward. But it didn't look like he was looking at anything. Chato poked him with his foot, yelling for him to get up. By now Chato was getting worried. Gordito was like a brother to him and he had never seen Gordito look like this.

A policeman saw Chato bending over Gordito; Chato was arrested. Gordito had died there naked on the grass outside the schoolyard trying to become a "man," trying to become a part of the gang. Chato had finally gone too far. The mixture of gasoline, the toxicity of the feces in his system, and the electric stimulation to his heart was too much for Gordito. They say he died instantly.

Chato went to prison. He was expelled from his gang. Getting caught was bad; getting arrested was a cardinal sin, unforgivable with no chance of ever rejoining the gang. Chato had no one to turn to.

Chato was sentenced to life in prison. He sat in the Youth Authority and then the Men's State Prison for five years before coming out of his shell. He doesn't talk much about those five years. He was so humiliated for being caught. He grieved for having killed his best friend. But after several years at the men's prison, he joined the group of men who made jeans. These men wielded scissors, needle and sewing machines and sewed jeans. Chato says it took many, many years to admit he loved sewing. He enjoyed the progression of cutting many layers of denim, of piecing and pinning the jeans together and finally sewing them into jeans. He thought they came out rather nicely.

It was not long after this that Chaplain Rique, also a Chicano, met Chato. Chaplain Rique was a former gang member who was now a priest. He visited the men in the prison and shared his personal story of a brother and father who were gang members, of a mother who had eleven children with nine different men, and another brother who died in a gang fight. Chaplain Rique knew what he was talking about; he had the stories and battle scars to show for it. The tattoo that covered his entire right calf was clearly visible when he swam laps at the prison pool. He talked to the men, got them to open up, and got them thinking about the past, present, and future. Many would never see a free day again, but some were on their way to being paroled. What would they do? How would they react? How would they resist temptation?

Chaplain Rique was a true friend, spending days at a time with these men. He loved them dearly and he told them that God loved them. But somehow he could never get it through Chato's head that he was forgiven. He cornered Chato and made him tell the tragic story of Gordito. The priest finally understood.

"You can never take back what you did. Gordito will never come alive again. But you are alive; you are walking and breathing. What are you going to do for the rest of your time here?"

It took many, many months of talking, but finally Chaplain Rique was able to convince Chato, whom he now called by his given name, Javier, to go with him to schools. The city's population was 83 percent Chicano. They needed one of their own to talk to them and share the realities of gang life. Chaplain Rique was proud to introduce Javier. And Javier talked and talked. He shared the temporary glory of belonging to a gang. He shared his story, his fears, and his despair. He shared how lonely it was in prison, how rough the others were, and what a terribly useless life he led. He did not mince his words; he was clear in his message: gangs were nothing to be glorified.

Javier is still sorry to this day. He knows that being sorry is no longer productive or good for anything, but he grieves his mistake. He also knows he has been forgiven. He is still in prison, but he visits many schools across the state, sharing his story and warning of the false lure of girls, drugs, and weapons. He feels if his experience can help just one person in the audience resist temptation, then it will be worthwhile.

Being A Servant

"Very truly, I tell you, servants are not greater than their master, nor are messengers greater than the one who sent them. If you know these things, you are blessed if you do them ... By this everyone will know that you are my disciples, if you have love for one another." (vv. 16-17, 35)

Danny looked at the document. He was standing at his secretary's desk. He scribbled something on the paper and threw it in front of her. "I need it today," he barked as he walked away. The door to his office slammed behind him.

Stacy hung her head. She worked hard and tried to do her work quickly, and still she felt like she was nothing more than a doormat. Danny worked long, long hours, but Stacy had a family. She worked ten hours and didn't even stop to take a lunch at times.

She tried her best at her work. She was an excellent speller and knew how to create a letter out of mumbled dictation. She was great at taking messages and remembering who was and wasn't in the office on a particular day. Why then did she feel so expendable? So useless?

Stacy talked to her husband and shared her frustration. She had worked for Danny a year, and in that year had only received one sincere, spontaneous compliment about her work. Stacy wasn't the type to go looking for compliments, but she needed to know if her work was acceptable, needed improvement, or just what her boss wanted. She had no way to tell.

So she resigned. Her boss was furious. "And just where will I get someone this late in the year?" he shouted at her. He fumed and stormed away. He turned toward her just before he reached his office. He told her to forget the two week notice. She could leave today.

Stacy couldn't believe it. So she *was* expendable. Disposable. She had been correct in her fears. She boxed up her stuff and walked out the door.

She drove out of the parking lot and suddenly, as she looked behind her, she felt a huge weight lifted from her shoulders. It was as if she were free. She didn't know what she was going to do next, but it wouldn't be taking a job anything like this, she promised herself. She headed for her husband's office. Maybe she could take him out to lunch.

Stacy enjoyed exactly three days of "freedom" as she called it. Then a friend called her and asked if she was interested in working for a lawyer who needed a competent, trusted secretary. Would she consider it? Stacy's knees felt weak. She would love to work, but what if the boss was rude? And what if he treated her like a dog? She wouldn't be able to stand it.

Her friend begged her. "Please, Stacy. You have my word. He is really, really nice. He is a faithful member of our church and I have worked with him on church council. I will bet my life on the fact that he will treat you fairly and kindly. Anyway, I threatened to sue him if he isn't nice to you...." Her friend laughed. "I was just kidding, Stacy. Give him a try. Just call him and talk to him."

So Stacy did. Her fingers trembled as she dialed the phone. "Hager Law Office" said a very friendly, older male voice. Stacy swallowed.

"Good afternoon. I'm looking for Ron Hager. This is Stacy Evensen." Stacy heard a whoop at the other end. "I knew it! I knew you would have a great telephone voice! Can you come and meet me today?" The man was excited. He was obviously Ron.

They met and they looked at each other. Ron explained that his wife was ill and she had been his only secretary over the last 37 years. He promised not to call Stacy "honey." He smiled at her. She decided she would help out for one week and then she would see if she wanted to continue.

"You drive a hard bargain. But for one week, at least I'll have a great secretary!" Ron was excited.

Ron made coffee in the morning and brought a mug to her. She was embarrassed, but Ron insisted that he only made coffee because the smell woke him up and he didn't want the pot to go to waste. Besides, he wanted to do that for her since she had graciously agreed to help him out just for the week. He smiled at her. The week flew by.

They worked together well. Ron asked her often to listen to an opening or closing argument. He wanted an honest critique. She decided to give her job a try for another week. And another week. Soon she had been there three months. Ron's wife recovered from her virus and came to work alongside Stacy. Stacy heard all about their five grandchildren and Ron in turn heard all about Stacy's three children.

Yes, they worked well together. There was mutual respect. There was mutual friendship.

A Religious Dilemma

*"Since it was the day of Preparation, the Jews did not
want the bodies left on the cross during the sabbath,
especially because that sabbath was a day of great so-
lemnity. So they asked Pilate to have the legs of the
crucified men broken and the bodies removed." (v. 31)*

Maia knew she was carrying twins. A single mother who does
not speak English, Maia knew something was wrong when her
doctor checked her out much more extensively at her 28-week
checkup. She didn't have the nursery quite ready and hoped the
twins hadn't decided to come into the world a little early. She still
needed those twelve weeks until their official due date to get things
ready.

Maia had already picked out names: Jessie and Joseph if they
were boys; Amanda and Bethany if they were girls; and Jessie and
Amanda if one of each. Dr. Gram looked worried when he listened
carefully to Maia's enormous belly. Dr. Gram's nurse spoke Spanish and she told Maia that Dr. Gram wanted to do some further
testing. She did not translate that Dr. Gram was indeed very, very
worried. He could detect only one heartbeat although the ultra-
sounds showed obvious twins. There was hardly any movement
when he gently pushed on Maia's stomach. The reactions were not
what he had expected or hoped for.

After extensive testing, Maia was told the babies would be taken
by Cesarean section. Maia was disappointed and called her boyfriend, mom, and two sisters. Maia was prepped for surgery and a
few hours later the babies were born.

Amanda and Bethany were hurried off to the Pediatric Intensive Care Unit. They were not only twins: they were joined at the

hip — literally. They were conjoined. When their cells split in gestation, somehow they stopped before they were finished completely splitting, and the girls grew that way. Their bodies were joined from the belly button down. It was quite a shock to Maia, but she was glad her mother and sisters could be with her. She would need an enormous amount of strength to face the days ahead.

Her boyfriend, Jimmy, hadn't wanted anything to do with the actual birth. He told her he was afraid of hospitals, since his mother died in one, and he would wait to hear the news. He was waiting at the body shop when he got the call to come to see the babies and Maia immediately. The doctor wanted to confer with the care team and would be with Maia and Jimmy later. They wanted Maia to have a chance to be in recovery and gather her strength.

The obstetrician, three pediatricians, a neonatologist, and a cardiovascular surgeon were called together and met for over an hour. Baby One, now named Amanda, was the stronger of the two and looked pink and healthy. Her Apgar score was seven. Baby Two, now called Bethany, was a little grayer, not responding appropriately to stimuli and had an Apgar score of two.

It appeared from the CT scan that Amanda's body was more complete than Bethany's. Amanda had a liver, kidneys, bladder, and the other necessary organs from the hip down. She had two legs.

Bethany was joined to Amanda at the belly button and she did not have a liver, kidneys, or other organs. Her body literally ended at her stomach. She did not have legs.

The case was very intense: the girls would have to be separated at once so that Amanda could be a viable little infant and have a better chance at normalcy. The doctors carefully outlined their thoughts to each other on how to disjoin the twins. The surgical team was enlisted, with orders given that they be put on standby immediately. Dr. Gram was still in attendance at the care conference even though he gave over the twins' care to the head of Neonatology, Dr. Smirna, a brilliant doctor. They were assured that physically Maia had come through the Cesarean very well. Their main concern now were the twins.

The operating room was scheduled, blood was ordered, and technicians were put on standby. Charts were quickly drawn up and scans were held up and compared, with various points carefully circled. But first the doctors needed Maia's permission, a technicality at best.

Dr. Smirna was introduced by Dr. Gram as they walked into the recovery room and closed the curtain around Maia and Jimmy. Through the interpreter, Dr. Smirna carefully explained the procedure to them, going over a few carefully selected scans of the girls' internal organs. They didn't want to overwhelm the parents, but they needed to know the intensity and gravity of the procedure before them. Bethany had no chance, but they wanted to ensure that Amanda was as good as she could be when she came out of surgery. A plastic surgeon would help once all the surgeries were complete for minimal scarring later on. Could the parents sign so the surgery could begin? They could have a chance to say goodbye to Bethany privately while the doctors got things ready.

Maia and Jimmy asked for some time alone, and it didn't take them long to decide. They would not allow their babies to be disjoined. They were not God and only God could make that decision. They would not choose which baby would live or die — that was up to God. They were devout in their beliefs, and something like this was not going to allow them to waver in their knowledge that God had a plan for them, for Amanda, and for Bethany. God would decide, not Maia and Jimmy.

Dr. Smirna was stunned when she returned and heard Maia's proclamation. She looked at the interpreter, asking if there was any question about what was going on. Were there any technical questions they had? Had they understood the enormous burden Amanda was under breathing for Bethany? Did they understand the urgency to get the twins apart?

The interpreter spoke with Maia. She was convinced Maia and Jimmy understood perfectly well what was going on and that only one could survive if disjoined. None would survive if left in their present state. Yet the parents felt that both were in God's care, and the parents refused to sign. Dr. Smirna rushed out, heading to the hospital legal department.

Round and round the doctors, social workers, lawyer, and ethicist went with the parents. All to no avail. They could not and would not allow anything to happen to their daughters that was not sanctioned by God. If one was to die, then one would die. If they were both to live, then God would allow them to live. If they were meant to die, then God would take them.

The hospital understood that the parents wanted to stick to their beliefs, but it was not content, and the state was called in to take immediate custody of the twins. They were disjoined at the age of four days. Bethany died during surgery. Amanda died four hours later of complications.

> *"Then the soldiers came and broke the legs of the first and of the other who had been crucified with him. But when they came to Jesus and saw that he was already dead, they did not break his legs. Instead, one of the soldiers pierced his side with a spear, and at once blood and water came out." (vv. 32-34)*

Doing Something — For God

"Set your minds on things that are above, not on things that are on earth, for you have died, and your life is hidden with Christ in God. When Christ — who is your life — is revealed, then you also will be revealed with him in glory." (vv. 2-4)

"Honey, I want to do something for God. What should I do?"

Bobby rubbed his eyes. It was 2:30 in the morning, and he had been sleeping soundly. Had been. He looked at Rosie to make sure she was really awake. He wanted to see if maybe after thirteen years of marriage she had taken up sleep-talking. Rosie was staring at him with her enormous brown eyes, holding her breath. "Well?" she said. Bobby looked at her again. She was fully awake; he sat up.

"What do you mean, sweetie? Like what?"

"Yea, like what could I do for God? I want to do something meaningful in my life." She looked in earnest at her beloved husband. She was dead serious.

Bobby stifled a yawn. He didn't want to be rude, and Rosie's tone sounded serious. He shifted to turn toward her.

"Well, like what? You sing in the choir. You usher, help with communion, and teach the high schoolers. Your banners hanging up by the altar are really pretty, sweetie. And what about all those casseroles that you always make for the new moms? Is that what you were thinking of?"

Rosie smiled. "No. I want to do something for God. You know. Something meaningful. Something *important*."

"Oh." Bobby didn't really know what to say. "What about our kids? They are great kids, even if I do say so myself. They're good at school. They love their sports and instruments. They have nice friends. That's something very special to me."

Rosie's eyes rolled upward in exasperation. "No, that's just because you're their father. I want to do something for God. *God.* You know."

Bobby was stumped. What could she mean? He fought back a yawn. "Well, sweetie peetie, I'm not sure I know what you're thinking about. You have nice friends yourself. You always keep the house so tidy, and I love it when our friends come over. I'm always so proud of you. That's important."

"No, that's for you, for them, for my own feeling," Rosie said. She sighed. "I want to do something meaningful. Something *important.*"

"Well, I don't know. Your work at the shelter is appreciated. And what about the layettes you help put together for the hospital? And people love your little blankets you sew up for the AIDS ward. That's important. Is that what you mean?"

Rosie looked at Bobby and began to yawn. "No, honey. I was thinking that's all for people. I want to do something important. Something for God. But what can it be? What should I do?"

Bobby was so tired his eyes almost crossed. He took his wife in his arms. "Sweetie, we'll have to think about it and ask God to help us think. In the meantime, why don't you just be yourself until you get an answer?"

He held her tight and she relaxed. He looked down at her. She was sleeping peacefully.

Doubt — A Difficult Thing To Overcome

"The genuineness of your faith — being more precious than gold that, though perishable, is tested by fire — may be found to result in praise and glory and honor when Jesus Christ is revealed. Although you have not seen him, you love him; and even though you do not see him now, you believe in him and rejoice with an indescribable and glorious joy, for you are receiving the outcome of your faith, the salvation of your souls."
(vv. 7-9)

Doubt, especially self-doubt, is difficult to overcome. Sometimes it is impossible. Kenny has dyslexia. He doesn't read things backwards; he has a reading and comprehension difficulty. If he hears something, he can remember it, but reading takes special concentration and the meaning of something comes with great difficulty.

Kenny tried to hide his dyslexia, doing manual labor and staying out of the limelight. But the manager of the warehouse where he worked had watched him and pegged him for a promotion. A big promotion. Mark wanted Kenny to be his assistant. Kenny was a very dedicated worker; he insisted on doing things over that were not to his liking and often stayed overtime to help gets things done at the huge plant. Kenny was an excellent worker.

When his manager offered Kenny a substantial raise and a promotion as assistant manager, Kenny was both honored and frightened. What if Mark found out he could hardly read? What if Kenny were required to write things? The offer so frightened him that the next day Kenny called in sick. The manager was confused. Why was Kenny not happy to take the position? Why had Kenny called in sick for the first time after six years on the job? What had Mark done wrong when he offered him the promotion? Was the raise not enough?

Mark called Kenny, but Kenny didn't answer the phone. He was too frightened. Finally Mark drove out to Kenny's modest home, climbed the stairs, and pounded on the door. Kenny answered the door and told Mark he could not take the promotion and that he was quitting in two weeks.

It was lucky for Kenny that his manager was a good, patient man. He told Kenny that if he quit, he would never be able to find another worker like him. Mark needed Kenny to help him watch over the workers. Kenny was trusted by the men and women who worked on the production line; they confided in him. The manager needed Kenny's honest input and opinions. They would work well together. He argued and argued with Kenny and finally told Kenny he could stay at his position as long as he liked, but that no one else would get the offer of assistant manager. Mark turned to walk away, but before he did so, he told Kenny he believed in him.

Kenny would never use the word sentimental to describe himself, but he was overcome with emotion as he headed back inside. Mark believed in him, that was obvious. But Kenny hardly believed in himself. He cried at the edge of his bed, asking God what to do. He sat there so long he became sleepy, and when he finally fell asleep Kenny dreamed of his role model, a famous man. Kenny had listened to audio tapes of all his work, his biography, and any interviews about him. Kenny idolized this man and so in his dream he found the answer.

Kenny's idol, Sparky, had a difficult childhood. Sparky had great difficulties in school: he failed almost every subject he took, and he didn't do well enough in sports to make any team. Basically ignored by his classmates, Sparky was neither outgoing nor socially adept. Sparky lived a mediocre life, being a nobody, not fitting in anywhere.

But Sparky did one thing and he did it very well. He loved to draw. And he was proud of his drawings. He had decided to become an artist, and even though the drawings submitted to his high school yearbook were rejected, Sparky was undeterred. He was going to be an artist.

83

Sparky was so confident in the only thing he did well that he wrote to Mr. Walt Disney. He told Mr. Disney that he was submitting a cartoon idea and asked him to consider it. His idea was promptly rejected.

Nevertheless, Sparky was going ahead with his drawings. He decided to showcase his mediocre life in cartoon form. He showed an average kid who didn't amount to much and who wasn't taken seriously by anyone. He drew his experience from his own point of view. He drew because he knew he was good at it, and he was going to continue to submit his cartoons until someone took them. He at least believed that much about himself.

And the world loved it. Sparky's comic strip, *Peanuts*, became more than a cartoon strip. It gave hope to others who were mediocre, who were underachieving, who were not likely to succeed. For fifty years, Charles Schulz was a hero by illustrating his hopes, dreams, frustrations, successes and rejections in drawings. Charles Schulz was admired because he wasn't afraid to explore his rejections and dejections on paper. Charles Schulz was a winner.

Kenny sat up. Charles Schulz, Sparky, believed in himself. Why couldn't Kenny? Trembling, Kenny went to his manager the next day, and they talked about Kenny's dyslexia, his inability to read well, and his poor writing skills. A deep bond was formed between the two men as they shared Kenny's most intimate secret, his point of sorrow, the issue that made him feel ashamed. His manager reassured Kenny that there was nothing to be ashamed of, Kenny could continue on the line part-time and part-time in the office, giving Mark needed feedback and reporting to Mark any inconsistency, danger, or irregularity he saw. Mark hired a part-time secretary for Kenny so Kenny could dictate notes and reports.

Kenny continued to be a dedicated worker, and eventually he hired three assistants to help him in his position of assistant manager. There are still times when Kenny has self-doubt, but Kenny knows God will love him no matter if he can read or write. Kenny has determination, grit, and a wonderful God.

He also has a great manager.

Unrecognized Faith

"When he was at the table with them, he took bread, blessed and broke it, and gave it to them. Then their eyes were opened, and they recognized him." (vv. 30-31)

Pastor Jim and his wife Ida were shaking hands with people as they came to church. Pastor Jim was idly chatting with several of the people as they quickly shook his hand and entered the massive building. Ida was standing beyond, sharing a story about the twins: they were so active, learning to walk and into everything! At two years of age, no one held Ida's heart more captive than her only grandchildren.

It was a cold, spring morning, with a little snow still on the ground. Jim was glad his alb was wool. He was just about to close the door against the wind when he saw an older man walk up the sidewalk. The man walked with a cane and had a limp. His coat was open, flapping in the wind. His suit underneath was wrinkled, his tie crooked. Pastor Jim smiled broadly and waved him on through the door. "Welcome!" Jim said in his booming, cheerful voice. He shook the man's hand and introduced himself as the pastor of First Church. The man said his name was Peter. Jim took Peter's coat and hung it up in the foyer and waved for an usher to help Peter find a seat. Jim's thoughts turned to the worship service.

His music minister did such a great job. As a daughter of a pastor, she was very familiar with integrating the music and the lectionary cycle: the hymns and special numbers fit the texts perfectly. He knew he was lucky to have this young lady on staff. He felt his heart soar as her prelude came to a close. He smiled at her.

The service was joyful and upbeat. His sermon was predictable: know God loves you, know God is with you, know that God cares for you. He wove stories into the sermon from his past as a missionary and people nodded and smiled at the right places. He caught sight of Ida and watched for a look of disapproval or approval. She was his meter and his true critic, and she didn't let Jim get away with much. She nodded and smiled. He hoped someone would be moved and someone would understand how much God loves them.

The special music was indeed special, and Pastor Jim said so. Chelsea was only twelve years old, but the music she made with her viola moved even his 55-year-old heart. He reminded the children how important they were in their church and what special gifts God had given each of them. He raised his hand to bless the church.

Pastor Jim caught sight of Peter, and he smiled at him. Peter. Who was he? Was he transient? Was he traveling? What was his story? His eyes stayed a second longer as he pronounced the benediction. "... The Lord look upon you with favor and give you peace."

Pastor Jim once again stood at the back, shaking hands with his parishioners and their visitors. He met Julie's boyfriend, the Hanson family's great-uncle, a doll named Betsy, and several members who were returning from their winter stay down south. He couldn't blame them; a warm climate could be so inviting at times when there were several inches of snow around! He shook hands again with Peter as he walked out of the church.

"That was a good message, Pastor. It warmed my heart." Pastor Jim and Ida chatted with Peter a while and invited him to lunch. Ida was thinking a hot meal might be good for Peter. Pastor Jim was thinking that Peter might be craving company. It would be good for all of them.

They went to a nearby restaurant and had what amounted to a Thanksgiving feast: turkey, dressing, potatoes, yams, vegetables, a salad bar, even several pies to choose from. What a banquet it was. They spoke about superficial things at first: Jim befriending his beloved Ida after World War II, their life on the missionary field, and the adventures as parents in Madagascar. They shared of their loneliness for their children when they were sent off to England for high school. There were plenty of stories about their younger son's two children: the twins. Soon their conversation turned deeper, with Peter sharing stories of his own travels across the world and the suffering he saw in many war-torn countries. Peter said that he was sorry to learn in his travels that so many people didn't know about Jesus. He only briefly mentioned that his wife died in childbirth, and he never talked about it again.

When they went to pay, it was Peter who handed the money to the waitress, much to the shock of Pastor Jim, who insisted that he had invited Peter and he expected to pay. But Peter would have none of it. "Maybe in the next few days or weeks we'll eat together again and it'll be on you. Right now I need to go home, I have a very special visitor coming."

And so began their friendship. Jim and Peter met several times at the café. Peter hardly ever talked about himself, though. He was adept at turning the conversation to Jim and evaded many direct questions. He loved it when Ida came to join them. He encouraged Ida's idea for a quilt design for the back wall of the church. He even felt free enough to debate points that Jim made in his sermons or in adult Bible study. Peter was an honest, seemingly carefree person, interested in others and his relationship with God — it turned out he also had a keen interest in the Bible. Jim bounced ideas off of Peter several times in preparation for a sermon or class. Their friendship was deepening.

It was quite a shock when Pastor Jim received a phone call from the hospital: Peter was in Intensive Care and was not expected to live much longer. Jim and Ida hurried to the hospital to be with their friend. Peter was on oxygen and had IVs in place. He looked ghostly pale, yet he smiled when he saw his friends.

Jim tried to make the moment lighter and kidded Peter about not even knowing him for six months and already it seemed like a lifetime. But Jim also could see Peter was tired, and Jim wanted to make the most of the moment. They held hands and sat together. Jim prayed with Peter, asking God to give comfort and peace.

The nurse came in and told them she would miss Peter. He had come to the University Hospital many times in the last seven years that he had this illness, but now he knew his time on earth was ending and he had wanted to be closer to the hospital. He had taken an apartment to be close by. Jim was so surprised. Never once in all their conversations had Peter mentioned he was ill. He had said he had traveled quite a bit, but Jim had never known if it was because he was transient or what the exact story was. It seemed although he had come to care deeply for Peter, he didn't really know who Peter was at all.

Peter's granddaughter came to visit. Her father had died of this same disease when she was only eighteen years old, and Peter was like a second father rather than a grandfather to her. She was his only family and she would miss him very, very much. She lived about an hour away and had come to visit him every Sunday afternoon without fail. She laughed when her grandfather rushed home one Sunday, was sorry he was late, but so excited about the pastor he had met! She knew all about Jim and Ida. Peter had told her everything about his new friends. He had been so happy to know them.

Peter died while holding Jim's hand. Jim wept for his friend and felt grief that he couldn't know Peter better. He admitted honestly to Ida he had cried for himself, too. He asked Peter's granddaughter if there was anything he could do with planning his funeral. She showed Jim the beautifully outlined worship service that Peter had planned. The music was beautiful; the texts were upbeat and confident. The tone of the service was one of faithfulness and celebration. Everything was ready. Peter had even penciled in Jim's name to do the benediction. Jim would do anything that she and Peter would want. "Just come to the church in our hometown, and please honor us by doing the blessing," was all she said. They parted with a hug.

Jim spent much time sitting with Peter, remembering their conversations, their pure and honest debates, the bond they had been building. He would indeed miss his friend.

When Jim and Ida set out for the funeral, they found the streets packed with cars. People were filing into Zion Church. Was this all for Peter? Their "simple" friend?

But Peter wasn't so simple at all. Peter had been a friend to hundreds in his home town. He was a philosophy professor who also had gone to seminary, not to be ordained but to give another focus to his philosophy studies. He spent every summer traveling in different parts of the world, traveling only with a small suitcase and relying on the goodness of people he met along the way. He in turn shared his faith with the people. Peter had only gotten in trouble once in his travels. He was in Pakistan, where Christianity is not something that is admitted to or shared with anyone. He was innocently sharing about Christ when he was arrested and jailed. He was beaten to the point of blackout until a guard felt pity on him and let him go. Peter had been to South America, Europe, Asia, Africa, the Scandinavian countries, and Russia. He had missed very few countries. Peter, this man who could debate so deeply with Jim. Peter, this man who so deeply loved Jesus that he was willing to risk his life sharing his faith story with others throughout the world. The pastor of Zion asked how many people could add such stories to their resume.

A fellow professor got up to speak. Peter was an activist, joining in protest against the unfair treatment of minority groups. He had been a beloved professor on campus, often letting students use his guest cottage if they had no place to go. He was a trusted colleague who was not afraid to challenge professors in their thinking. Jim nodded in understanding.

The congregation laughed when a young man shared how Peter had loaned him his only suit: a hopelessly outdated suit that the young man politely turned down. So Peter gave him a hundred dollars to buy a new suit. Peter, this simple man, who spoke, dressed, and acted simply. Many people spoke at the funeral about how he had given them money to buy food, clothing, or cars. He had even sponsored several young people with college funds.

Peter would be missed. He had given all his earthly possessions away about a year before when he knew his illness was progressing. He didn't want or need much anymore. He just wanted to be himself.

Jim got up to give the benediction. It was all he could do to keep from crying as he looked out over the large church. "And now may the Lord bless you...." It was packed with others who truly loved Peter. He turned to the casket: "... The Lord look upon you with favor and give us peace. Amen."

Easter 4
John 10:1-10

The Importance Of Sheep

" 'Very truly, I tell you, anyone who does not enter the sheepfold by the gate but climbs in by another way is a thief and a bandit. The one who enters by the gate is the shepherd of the sheep. The gatekeeper opens the gate for him, and the sheep hear his voice. He calls his own sheep by name and leads them out. When he has brought out all his own, he goes ahead of them, and the sheep follow him because they know his voice. They will not follow a stranger, but they will run from him because they do not know the voice of strangers.' " (vv. 1-5)

In Palestine, the shepherd figure was a familiar one: shepherds were part of the scenery, part of their world. A shepherd spent much time with his flock, caring for them and keeping watch over them. Many shepherds started watching sheep when they were very young, only to continue to be shepherds for the rest of their lives.

So familiar were the sheep with the shepherd that they knew their master's voice. The shepherd's duty was to guide the sheep to fresh water and pasture, to guard them from wild animals, and to lie across the entrance of the sheepfold at night. The shepherd was literally the door to the sheep.

In the biblical era it was a common practice to have slaves. Many early Christians were slaves, household or domestic servants. Slaves were often people of culture and education. Sometimes they were even superior to the masters, being doctors, philosophers, librarians, secretaries, musicians, or teachers. A slave had no legal rights, being a "thing" rather than a person, and servants were meant to obey. This was true not only when the master was generous and considerate but also when he was cruel and unfair. If the servants could not please their masters, they could at least try to please their

90

god, or in the case of Christian slaves, God, who understood their plight. Their motive for service then became a way of pleasing God, not their master. Their suffering is meritorious because Christ suffered for us, leaving an example to follow.

Hanukkah was instituted in 164 B.C. by Judas Maccabeus to rededicate the Temple that was defiled when Antiochus Epophanes offered upon its altar a sacrifice to Zeus. The festival took place in mid-December with a ceremony of lights. Some of the high priests at that time were fanatical and tyrannical, and this created a schism among the priest-kings.

When Jesus came around to the Temple, the Temple was supervised and controlled by wealthy, aristocratic families. They were very unpopular, since they were conservative in religion and liberal in their lifestyle. They were not a good example of being exemplary pastors of the Lord's flock.

The Old Testament ideal of a shepherd, or head of the church, was one of gentleness, nurturing, and wisdom. God is the shepherd of Israel, the one who would lie at the door of the sheepfold, watching out for them and caring for them. God's chosen ones, then, are the nation's shepherds; but Jesus comes to say he is the one, true shepherd.

Thus, in this passage from John, Jesus refers to the good shepherd and the feast celebrating the purifying of the Temple. Jesus refers to the Roman persecutors as the "wolves," false teachers as the "hirelings," and all pretenders as the "thieves and robbers." But Jesus, who is willing to lay down his life for the sheep, is the true shepherd. Jesus has a close, personal relationship with each of his followers, who have absolute security and confidence in him. Jesus' care for his flock is unfailing, his company constant, his guidance supreme, and his love sacrificial. Jesus is the only True Shepherd.

What Good Can Come Of This?

―――――――

" 'Do not let your hearts be troubled. Believe in God, believe also in me. In my Father's house there are many dwelling places. If it were not so, would I have told you that I go to prepare a place for you? And if I go and prepare a place for you, I will come again and will take you to myself, so that where I am, there you may be also. And you know the way to the place where I am going.' " (v. 1)

Their hearts were troubled. They couldn't believe it. Six hours ago they had said good-bye to their son, Kyle, wishing him a fun evening with his friends. Kyle was on his way to a pizza parlor where his friends were gathering to watch a college football game. They had their pizza and then the group decided to go to the home of one of the boys. The boy's parents were gone for the evening and plans were made. They could watch the game from the huge television in the recreation room and help themselves to the well-stocked bar.

Kyle's parents were confused. Kyle didn't like the taste of alcohol and he never bragged about drinking to his friends. How was it that he had died on the couch at his friend's house? The doctors called it alcohol poisoning: the actual poisoning of the body by excessive drinking. Kyle wasn't an experienced drinker, and the combination of wine, liquor, and beer had erupted into a violent volcano inside his body, only to explode with life-taking force.

Kyle's parents were devastated. They were in shock as they went about making plans for the funeral. Their pastor and church friends were very supportive, yet they couldn't possibly understand. Kyle's parents lived in a closed world for the next three months as they grieved the loss of their bubbly, out-going son. They were sinking in despair.

One afternoon a teacher came to visit. She had heard about Kyle's death. She told them she could never understand what they had gone through — or were going through, but she was genuinely sorry about their loss. The teacher asked the parents to come and speak to the senior class. They were making plans for the senior high prom and, as their advisor, she wanted to give them an opportunity to hear Kyle's story. Would Kyle's parents consider it? Could they share openly the tragic story of alcohol poisoning?

Kyle's parents prayed about it and spoke to their pastor. Their pain was too deep, yet the opportunity to share was too tempting. Kyle's parents spoke — and the young people listened. The parents answered questions as they openly talked about the simple facts: too much alcohol will poison the body. They begged the youngsters to consider what their limit might be. Kyle's parents cried as they told his story, but they also laughed as they shared Kyle's funnier moments.

Over the years, Kyle's parents continued to speak to senior classes in the area and eventually around the state and country. Time was helping them. Speaking about their tragedy was also helping them. Kyle's parents were healing. They were able to share Kyle's memory with countless teens. They celebrated his life even as they mourned his death. And slowly they saw that although there was no way to undo what Kyle had done, maybe there was a way to give meaning to his legacy.

They hand out fliers, make buttons, and run television ads. Schools, youth organizations, and churches invite Kyle's parents to speak. They help spread the word about alcohol poisoning. They help others become aware. They also helped themselves ease their grief. They know Kyle is with God, for God had prepared a place for all of them. But while his parents are still on earth, they will carry out a mission to avoid another tragedy such as this.

The Advocate

---

*" 'The Father will give you an Advocate, to be with
you forever. This is the Spirit of truth, whom the world
cannot receive, because it neither sees him nor knows
him.' " (vv. 16-17)*

A new baby boy: Jonathan Richard. His family, friends, and pastor were there when the baby was born, and they were all excited at the birth! Paul felt so proud as he drove home to rest. It had been a long day. Paul smiled as he thought of his new baby boy.

But something was not quite right. During the night, Jonathan was taken to Children's Hospital "as a precaution — to check him out." Pamela was not alarmed, so Paul stayed with her a while before going to see Jonathan.

At Children's Hospital, Paul was told to scrub up. Jonathan wasn't just there as a precaution; the pediatrician told Paul that Jonathan had a serious heart problem. A pediatric cardiologist, Dr. Kegel, was summoned. Paul waited. Pastor Johnsen offered prayers, and the family gathered around, waiting.

After a time, Dr. Kegel came to speak to Paul and gave him the overwhelming news: the greater vessels in Jonathan's heart were transposed. The arteries were supposed to be crossed like an "X" to allow the blood to circulate through the body; instead, the arteries were not crossed and they were pumping the blood in a circle.

Paul was given his options and told to make a decision very quickly; there was no time to waste with Jonathan's heart in its present condition. Pastor Johnsen assured Paul and Pamela of his support — in whatever decision they made, whatever the outcome. Pastor Johnsen prayed that the Holy Spirit would be present to give guidance and peace during this stressful time.

Jonathan was not even twelve hours old. Pamela was prepared by the hospital staff to be moved to Children's Hospital to be at Jonathan's side and to help Paul make this tremendous decision. What should they do? Paul and Pamela's family never left their side. They spoke to Pastor Johnsen. Then they spoke again to the doctor.

There were two options: one would be to operate and make more holes between the ventricles to allow the blood to get through. The procedure was an old one, and the chances of dying on the operating table were very slim — but life expectancy was short: about twenty years. Jonathan would probably be sickly and weak most of his short life.

The other option, called the Norwood or Mustard Procedure, would sever, switch, and correctly reattach the aorta and pulmonary arteries. There was risk, with a twenty percent chance of Jonathan dying on the operating table. About 200 of these surgeries had been done — the oldest survivor was only six months old — and there was no real history or long-term effects documented. He either would or wouldn't make it. If Jonathan survived, he would probably lead a normal, healthy life.

It was a big decision, but one that only Paul and Pamela could make. And they made it quickly and confidently. They decided to do the Norwood Procedure and take the risk. If it would work, then they wanted Jonathan to have a normal life.

An air ambulance to Children's Hospital of Philadelphia was arranged. The $13,000 needed to charter the Lear Jet appeared miraculously and Paul, Pamela, Jonathan, a nurse, a doctor, and two pilots were on their way. Jonathan was only three days old.

The jet got to the airport late in the night and an ambulance rushed Jonathan to the hospital. That morning Paul and Pamela met with Dr. Norwood, and the consultation team reassured them that they had made a good decision.

The surgery was scheduled for the next morning. Paul and Pamela waited and the social worker periodically checked in with the doctors. After four hours, Dr. Norwood himself told them that Jonathan couldn't have done better: his tiny heart had tolerated the surgery extremely well. It was a success!

Paul and Pamela feel that prayers and the guidance of the Holy Spirit sustained them through the whole ordeal — and gave them the wisdom to make the awesome decision they needed to make so quickly. They are especially thankful for the support of Pastor Paul Johnsen, and for his reminder to put the whole situation in the hands of God.

Today Jonathan is a healthy sixteen-year-old. He plays basketball, baseball, soccer, violin and piano and loves *Star Trek* and *The Phantom of the Opera*. He rides a mountain bike and enjoys seafood.

Ascension Of Our Lord
Ephesians 1:15-23

A Prayer And A Blessing

"I have heard of your faith in the Lord Jesus and your love toward all the saints, and for this reason I do not cease to give thanks for you as I remember you in my prayers." (vv. 15-16)

Pastor Wallace was loved by many, many people. He had come to a rural, agricultural area and stayed for 41 years. He and his wife Bea had four children, three of whom would become pastors themselves. The fourth was a missionary teacher in Madagascar. Pastor Wallace's second and last call was to another rural church he started only thirty miles away. He stayed fifteen years. His reputation was tough but fair; disciplined but compassionate; strong but just.

Pastor Wally, as he was known, knew his time on earth was short. He was suffering from lung cancer and he wanted to say good-bye. But how does one say good-bye to old friends? Pastor Wally asked that a worship service be held the coming fall to celebrate the harvest and his eightieth birthday. Plans were being made; it was to be held at his first church.

Pastor Wally was excited. But he was also getting weaker and weaker. It was two months before the service, and he wanted it to be a success. He called his granddaughter, a pastor almost 200 miles away, to help him write the service. Could two of his sons also come and help him? The four collaborated about the litany, focusing on the harvest and the change of seasons from living, yielding crops, to the earth becoming quiet, dormant, and restful. They wrote a poem about being eighty — not so old, yet not so young either. They wrote the outline for the bulletin together.

Several church members helped get the church ready: the gutters needed to be straightened, the furnace cleaned and readied for the winter, and the front steps needed to be redone. The crack in the wall behind the altar could be fixed and the vestry needed to be cleaned out. There was great anticipation in the air. It was as if they were preparing for a festival.

Women got out scrapbooks and church records. They would make up a little play about notable events when Pastor Wally was their pastor. Like the time he arrived at the church an hour late when he forgot to set his clock. The people had waited patiently but the potluck dinner looked a little limp. They recalled the Sunday when his youngest son had let their new puppy into the church basement during an ice storm and afterward the frightened little dog wouldn't come out from under the basement steps.

There were many great memories. Pastor Wally had been with them through a flood, several tornadoes, deaths, births, baptisms, confirmations, and weddings. He had held their hands when people succumbed to illness, were torn with addictions, and made moves. He was their friend, their pastor, their confidante.

The time got closer and wheat bundles, corn stalks, pumpkins, squash, Indian corn, and other vegetables were arranged at the base of the altar. A banner was made decorated with leaves in red, yellow, gold, and orange falling downward. The pews were oiled and the rugs shampooed. They were ready.

It was a wonderful worship service. The organist was glowing as she played a special number. The litany went well, but his daughter had to lead it: Pastor Wally was just too weak. One grandson sang "How Great Thou Art," and a son read a poem about life as a "PK." It was hilarious. The synod bishop, who had been a classmate with Pastor Wally at seminary, gave the sermon. Finally, it was time for Pastor Wally to give the prayers. He stood up slowly. With great difficulty, he walked to the lectern and said a prayer, giving thanks to God for good memories, good friends, and good times. He thanked God for the guidance he had received as a young pastor, the strong support from his loving wife, for the vision his mentor had when Wally first came to the prairie, and for the opportunity to stay so long among the people. He was truly grateful for the many blessings he had. He encouraged the people in his prayer to continue praying for one another and to pray for their church leaders. "Prayer," he said, "is the most effective part of being a

Christian. You can pray for people you know or don't know. You can lift people up even when you can't do anything else for them. It is what has sustained me over all these years."

Pastor Wally asked the people to stand and he raised his hands. "And now may the Lord bless you and keep you, my good friends. May the Lord make his face shine radiantly upon you and be gracious to you as you have been gracious to me. The Lord look upon you with favor and give you a peace that passes all understanding deep within your hearts. Go in peace and serve the Lord!"

The closing hymn sounded a little quieter than usual as people sniffed quietly and choked back tears. They knew Pastor Wally was tired and very ill: he was going to be missed. It had taken a tremendous amount of energy, but Pastor Wally had given the church two very important gifts: a prayer and a blessing. And a chance to say good-bye.

The Sewage Pit

"Humble yourselves therefore under the mighty hand of God, so that he may exalt you in due time. Cast all your anxiety on him, because he cares for you. Discipline yourselves, keep alert. Like a roaring lion your adversary the devil prowls around, looking for someone to devour. Resist him, steadfast in your faith, for you know that your brothers and sisters in all the world are undergoing the same kinds of suffering. And after you have suffered for a little while, the God of all grace, who has called you to his eternal glory in Christ, will himself restore, support, strengthen, and establish you. To him be the power forever and ever. Amen." (vv. 6-11)

I was at a Michael Card concert many years ago, enjoying the message and the music of this fine musician and master of words. During an intermission time, Michael Card shared a story with us about a Chinese man who was punished because he declared that he believed in Jesus Christ.

Some of the details will surely be left out (my apologies), but the story is basically as follows. A man had heard about Jesus. He wanted to know more about this person named Jesus. He found a Bible, which is not allowed in China, and he read it. He read it with great interest and began to memorize passages. He felt something very different inside when he read the Gospel accounts, and he felt he could trust the words before him. He learned many things from the Bible: to pray, to meditate on the passages, and to keep sections deep within his heart. He knew he was a changed man, and he knew that somehow the memorization would someday help him.

The Chinese government to this day does not allow Bibles to be distributed or read or the Christian church to be acknowledged.

Back when this man discovered Christianity, it was even worse. Word got out that this man was behaving strangely: he was happy, he was peaceful, and he was encouraged about the future. He was interrogated by the police, and the man admitted he had found Jesus Christ and had been saved from eternal death.

The Chinese were not happy. They sentenced him to prison with heavy physical labor his punishment. But still the man was cheerful. He knew he might die in prison, but he felt he had nothing to lose. He shared his knowledge of Jesus with others, much to the outrage of his captors. The man was sentenced to the worst possible punishment: he would have to stir the sewage pit. Many died doing this job because of the disease, intense work, and lack of fresh air and water.

Stirring the sewage pit was horrific work. The goal was for the liquid to be able to drop down through a pipe to be filtered and cleaned. The solid part would have to be stirred and skimmed to another partition across that wall. The sewage had to be stirred and shoveled fifteen hours a day so that it would not harden.

For fifteen hours a day this man had to stir sewage. It was terrible work, but he persevered. After about seventeen years of stirring sewage, his case came under review of the prison officials, and he was allowed to be free. They were actually quite annoyed to hear his constant singing and talking. It seemed a miracle that he was even alive! He joined up with a missionary team and began speaking about his ordeal.

The man doesn't really call it an ordeal. He calls it an "opportunity." While in the pit, the man made up songs about the words he had read in his Bible. He spoke the words aloud from the Bible. He made up prayers, often praying for his captors and others who didn't yet know about Jesus. He remembered passage after passage, all the while stirring the sewage.

Few of us will ever know what the man is talking about. We can't relate to the punishment he had to endure. We can't even try to fathom the repulsion of a sewage pit, much less of having to be in it for fifteen hours a day. No, we can't really relate. We have freedom to express ourselves and to share what we learned in church or church school. We go to worship freely and we sing aloud. But

101

there are millions of people in many parts of the world who do not have this freedom.

But there is hope for China. Several Christian groups have organized themselves into bands of witnesses, literally walking and biking across China. They leave tracts which tell about Jesus. They wear specially-designed vests which accommodate carrying several small Bibles. They flood towns with Bibles and pamphlets during the middle of the night and then board a bus or train to go to another town so they will not get caught by the police. They are making headway. No one knows true numbers or what effect the tracts and Bibles are having, but estimates are as low as two million and as high as six million people who profess to be Christian.

There is hope for China.

Pentecost Day
1 Corinthians 12:3b-13

Niceties Don't Sell

*"Now there are varieties of gifts, but the same Spirit;
and there are varieties of services, but the same Lord;
and there are varieties of activities, but it is the same
God who activates all of them in everyone." (vv. 4-6)*

During the time of the Christian church in Corinth, a trance-like state testified to the fact that you were a Christian. Or if you had strange or ecstatic speech, you were considered a devout believer. Why? If you had a spectacular gift, you were considered gifted by God.

It's true that the greasy wheel gets the oil. The more sensational stories make the headlines. But there are truly devout, deeply spiritual people who never get one moment's notice, yet they possess unparalleled gifts from God. They also have spiritual gifts.

Marsha's church group has quietly been making hundreds of quilts every year to be sent overseas with a world relief organization. Three times a week, ladies get together to chat, sew, and piece quilts together from donated fabrics. The fabric is ironed, put onto long tables, and then cut into large squares. They are sewn together with other coordinating colors. The ladies also use donated clothing that is no longer in style. A team works quietly at home taking out seams and converting the articles into fabric pieces. Another team works diligently cutting and ironing these into smaller, usable squares. A large group gets together the first and third Tuesday of the month to transform quilt tops into finished quilts.

Marsha is proud of her group's efforts. In the 23 years they have been getting together in the church basement, they have sent almost 12,000 quilts for missions and world relief. Seventeen hundred smaller quilts have been made for church baptisms and to be donated to the local children's hospital AIDS wing.

Marsha has never been in the newspaper. She doesn't expect to be nor does she seek to be in the newspaper. But what is curious is that when a new youth director had a sexual misconduct charge brought against him, it was all over the paper. Her church became known for the alleged deed of this young man. It made Marsha sad. She wished the news focused on all the good her church did.

But goodness doesn't sell.

Rod's church has been working with neighboring Presbyterian and Reformed Church in America congregations as they joined efforts to build a youth center in the old theater building. There is a computer room with five computers that young people can use for an hour at a time. There are several tape recorders and CD players with countless headphones lying on the floor.

The theater's seats were taken out, and the floor lends itself well as a huge recreation room. There is a pool table to the side and five vending machines dispense anything from crackers to chips and juice to pop. Dances are held in the theater basement.

The three church groups have been working together quite successfully. Each of the churches took turns painting and decorating a different area of the theater. Four of the dads built a long skateboard ramp. Several moms helped make curtains and tablecloths. An area nursery donated several trees and hedges for the side lawn. There is an outdoor roller rink adjacent to the theater with bright lights that stay on until 10 p.m. Three basketball hoops wave in the breeze.

The youth center has not been featured outside their small local newspaper. But when their respective governing church bodies discussed the Call to Common Mission, it was front page news, featuring all the concerns each side had. Rod's friends didn't understand. How could their churches start and effectively run a youth center in their own town when their national church groups were portrayed in the news as "bickering" and "constantly in-fighting"? Rod wished the youth center were the focus of the media.

But harmony doesn't sell.

Niceties don't sell newspapers or television news spots. It is much more interesting and a better seller when sexual misconduct or fighting is featured. Issues of race, homosexuality, and the like garner much attention. Issues of disaster relief, homelessness, and youth programs don't.

Still, Marsha and Rod persevere. As do countless others. They are not after media attention. They wish to show the face of a faithful community. They will continue to show anyone who might look for the face of God's love, grace, and mercy. Niceties don't sell; but niceties shape the way believers behave.

Holy Trinity
Genesis 1:1—2:4a

From Chaos To Harmony

"In the beginning when God created the heavens and the earth, the earth was a formless void and darkness covered the face of the deep, while a wind from God swept over the face of the waters." (vv 1:1-2)

The children — aged nine through thirteen — were milling around waiting for the old school bell that hung outside to ring. They had been playing in the playground near the lake when someone mentioned there were only ten minutes left before they had to go. They were running toward the top of the hill. Suddenly, a shrill sound filled the air as the director sounded the bell three times. Ninety children ran inside and scrambled to their seats in the auditorium.

Avis, their director, gathered them by age, then ordered their seating by various abilities. She had them sing a refrain from a popular song heard on the radio. Everyone knew it, and everyone sang eagerly and loudly. Yet they sang in different keys, with differing tempos and the sound was shrill.

Avis turned to them. "You all sang beautifully in your own way. But if we want to sing together, we have to work together. Let's go outside and play and learn to work together."

The children looked happy as they ran outside. They shrieked when they saw the parachute game. Choir camp was going to be such fun!

They did have lots of fun; but they also worked hard that week. They were together six hours a day. Several musicians worked with the children: flautists, pianists, guitarists, even a violinist. The children paired off for singing lessons, went in groups of six for section practice, and sang together in groups of twenty or so. They made their voices match the piano, a pitch pipe, the guitar, the violin and a flute. They sang high; they sang low. They sang scales; they sang popular songs. They breathed deeply; they sang in front of candles, taking care not to blow them out.

They played together, worked together, and most of all, listened to each other as they sang. And they got better and better. What at first came out as a chaotic bunch of notes sung in all kinds of keys was turned into a sweet harmony timed to the tapping of Avis' stick.

The children knew they had worked hard. But they had had such fun! And they knew they sang beautifully. They were excited for the concert they would put on that Friday. Avis said she didn't work miracles; she just took different little twigs and branches to make a glorious tree.

A glorious, singing tree!

Doing The Right Thing

" 'Everyone then who hears these words of mine and
acts on them will be like a wise man who built his house
on rock ... And everyone who hears these words of mine
and does not act on them will be like a foolish man who
built his house on sand.' " (vv. 24, 26)

Len and Jeanne are the epitome of "good parents" according
to their four sons, who keep in close contact. They raised the sons
to be self-sufficient (something their wives appreciate!). They incorporated their faith in their lifestyle, helping others in time of
need and giving generously to church and charities alike. Len and
Jeanne didn't talk much about their faith: they simply live it.

They will probably not go down in history for any single event,
but they are well-loved in their large church, which they helped
start. Len was the first congregation president and Jeanne spent
hours and hours helping at their new church, doing whatever needed
to be done.

Today three of their sons are pastors and the youngest is a successful sales manager in a manufacturing plant. While they get a
little embarrassed about their pastor-sons and declare, "What have
we done wrong?" Len and Jeanne are proud of all four of their
sons. They don't care what their occupations are: they care what
their sons' private lives are like. They always preached that empty
spiritual gestures are just that: empty. They care about what is in
their sons' hearts.

When the boys were teenagers, their mother had surgery and
was in great pain. It hurt them to see Jeanne in such tremendous
agony, crawling to the bathroom and not being able to lie, sit, or
stand comfortably. Jeanne endured major surgery to fuse two
vertebrae.

Several years after the surgery, Jeanne was still in pain and unable to get rid of numbness in her leg. When she went to the doctor for in-depth testing, she was told the surgery that was performed was not successful. In fact, the surgeon who performed the surgery was being sued for malpractice. Many people were filing a class action suit against the doctor. It seems the doctor performed several unnecessary surgeries.

Jeanne was contacted and asked if she wanted to be a part of the suit. She didn't take long to refuse to take part in it. Although the doctor was wrong, Jeanne didn't want to be compensated for something she couldn't prove. She just didn't feel it was right.

The doctor was found negligent and the suit participants won. Some might argue that Jeanne was mistaken not to take the money offered. While Jeanne can see their point, she feels she needs to do what is right for her and her convictions. She doesn't want anything to do with money gained from a lawsuit. It won't change her situation; it won't replace her ailing back.

Jeanne is still in constant pain, but she has many diversions: she quilts and keeps a small garden in the back yard. Her sons and grandchildren visit often and — as she would say — Len keeps her busy. Jeanne did what was right for her. She is not into pretense. She would rather quietly live out her faith in her daily life, helping, serving, and being faithful.

Proper 5/Ordinary Time 10
Matthew 9:9-13, 18-26

The Reluctant Follower

"As Jesus was walking along, he saw a man called Matthew sitting at the tax booth; and he said to him, 'Follow me.' And he got up and followed him." (v. 9)

I wonder what Matthew felt like when Jesus said, "Follow me." Was it suprising? Was it scary? Did it make him angry? Did Matthew follow Jesus right away? Or did Matthew have to digest this request...?

At the risk of offending people, I have to say that when my husband was assigned to a certain area of the country, I was the most reluctant follower God has probably ever seen. Well, the most reluctant *wife*, for sure!

We had both finished our seminary studies, and my husband was waiting for a call to be assigned to a particular area — we didn't know where we would end up. We were home in California, and David was serving as interim pastor at a nearby church. David had said on those "mobility forms" that he wanted to be in the southwest to be close to our aging parents. He mentioned that he desired to be in a Hispanic area so that I could continue in Hispanic ministries. South. West. We didn't think that was so difficult.

We were excited at the possibilities. Maybe we would be called close to home in southern California, or maybe even Nevada or Arizona — we love the desert! Perhaps Colorado — oh, how we love mountains! Or Texas where countless positions are advertised requesting help in Hispanic ministries. We didn't think too much about it: David had his interim ministry, and I was busy being a case worker for Spanish-speaking families who had children with developmental disabilities. That was my job before I left for seminary, and I was honored when they took me back as a senior bilingual case manager. I loved my job, my co-workers, and the chance to minister to people in need — all the while speaking Spanish! I was very happy.

I remember the day so well when a certain synod bishop called. I'll never forget it, as a matter of fact. It's as if it were this morning. I was expecting — about six weeks along — and was excited about our second child. My thoughts were much more on the baby than on anything else. I had just come home from going to garage sales and had seen a beautiful oak crib. I was telling my husband about it when the telephone interrupted us.

I only heard David's end of the conversation. I didn't need more than that to figure out what was happening. "Hello? Yes, this is David Berg. Yes, we are settling in at Reformation. Yes, the Korean church is getting a new pastor, and we are excited to have him come! Hmmmm. Yes. Oh! Oh? Western North Dakota? Oh! Well, do you have a large Hispanic community there? Oh, ... only three or four families in the entire area are Hispanic? I don't understand. Oh. We're assigned to Western North Dakota then. Well, how did that happen? No, no, I'll be glad to receive their phone call and talk to them. Yes, between Bismarck and Minot. Oh, I'll be sure to share this with Con. I'll call you back later this week ... Nice to talk to you too ... Have a good afternoon."

I sat down. I gave David a strange look as he continued to stare at the phone in his hand. He didn't look right at me. "David. What is it?" David shared the fuller conversation with me. We had been assigned to Western North Dakota. I couldn't believe it.

My emotions ran the gamut from happy to get a call to outraged that our request for an opportunity for my ministry to be considered was ignored to understanding that there was such a great need for pastors in the rural areas of the country. David explained that it just wouldn't really look good for a new pastor to refuse an area assignment. He asked me to consider it.

Wow! In a three-minute phone call, my life was turned upside down. Forget about being close to family. Forget about Hispanic ministries. Forget about continuing a career — the bishop had said the area was very rural. I had to take several deep breaths in the ensuing months as I experienced anger (I hate the process — the bishop doesn't even know us and he's making us move so far!) to grief (what about my chance for a career?) to depression (I'll be so homesick and will feel so isolated). I was so distraught that I lost the baby I was carrying. I was even more outraged at the feeling of being forced into this.

David brought me out of my depression. He sat me down one day and asked if I could consider a short call, and then he would move anywhere I needed to go so that I could pursue my career. I thought I loved him a great deal, but that day I loved him even more. We prayed about this move together. We talked (and talked!) to experienced pastors — both who had to go long distances and short. We talked to our parents and brothers and sisters. Finally, we were ready to say, yes, David could consider a call. I could concentrate on our daughter and would find something to do. We called the bishop back.

The bishop had eyed a certain church but the pastor hadn't announced his resignation to the congregation yet. Once the pastor announced his resignation, we had to wait for the church profile and papers to be submitted. Everything took time — lots of time. It was six months before the process was complete and we could talk "call." On David's birthday, we went to North Dakota to "look around."

What beauty! I had never seen anything so beautiful in my life. Vast, open fields buried in snow. We saw an eagle the first day we were there, flying low above what looked like an iced-over lake. A big snow owl was sitting on the fence watching us as we pulled up to the home of one of the call committee presidents. We stayed for four days and it was both interesting to see the land, exciting to meet the kind people, and great to spend time with two deeply caring, committed call committee presidents: Larry and Myron. They loved their parish, they loved the parsonage, and they were committed to finding a pastor.

The whole process took eight months. By the time the church could have us, we were ready and eager to go. We had a great time driving cross-country, showing our daughter Kjrstin the Grand Canyon and other interesting places along the way. We added layer upon layer as we headed farther north. It was very exciting!

Now when I look back at that time, I thank God for the chance to have those eight months to prepare mentally for the challenge ahead and to adjust to the transitions I would have to make. I also wonder what God thought of me. Not the most willing follower, huh? But God didn't give up on me! In North Dakota, I had opportunities to write, to tutor third- and fourth-year Spanish students and to come home every now and then. I had close friends inside and outside the parish. I learned so much from our first call. Practical things like how to plant and harvest, can food, survive in winter storms, and do Hardanger embroidery. And I learned more important things like trusting in God to put us in the right place as He watched over us in rural North Dakota.

This reluctant follower finally felt a deep sense of peace on the great northern plains: I knew I had to be where I was at that time in my life. We gained much in David's first call: patience with each other, trust in God, and a deeper level of communication with our family. We received many gifts while we were on the western side of North Dakota: friendship, patience, understanding, humor, and countless other blessings.

But the greatest blessing for me personally came nine months after we arrived: a son named Andrew!

Their Vow Of Poverty

---

*"When he saw the crowds, he had compassion for them,
because they were harassed and helpless, like sheep
without a shepherd. Then he said to his disciples, 'The
harvest is plentiful, but the laborers are few; therefore
ask the Lord of the harvest to send out laborers into his
harvest.' " (vv. 36-38)*

I grew up in a predominately Catholic town, and I have three
friends who are priests. I admire their adherence to the vows they
took at their ordination: a vow of obedience, a vow of celibacy, and
a vow of poverty. Each took their vows quite seriously at their ordination and still do to this day.

Ronny, as I know him, grew up the oldest of six sons. Unknown to him until after his ordination, Ron's mother had promised at his baptism that her oldest son would become a priest. Ron
loved helping out at the church as a youngster and never considered any other profession. His undergraduate degrees in Philosophy, Religion and Education were all geared for his seminary training and subsequent ordination into the priesthood. He never questioned his calling.

But Ron ran into an unexpected problem. Ron was tempted by
a dear childhood friend of ours, a beautiful woman who was deeply
involved with the Roman Catholic church. She taught Rite of Christian Initiation classes to adults, made beautiful paraments, and
chaired the annual carnival festivities. She was also drop-dead gor-
geous. It was very difficult for Ronny to work closely with Kelly,
and finally he asked his bishop — a good friend — for a call to be
transferred. He loved Kelly, but he loved his vocation more, and he
did not want to jeopardize all that his family and friends sacrificed

for his seminary education. He sought counseling to deal with his feelings, spoke truthfully with his beloved bishop, and was soon transferred to a parish in the Southwest. It was what saved his profession, he says now. He still loves Kelly as a friend, but her marriage to a kind man gave him some closure. He is grateful how events turned out.

Jerry is funny and smart. He is very handsome and, in a way, he can't help but realize it. He takes care to dress meticulously. His shirts are pressed to perfection, his trousers are only the best wools, and his shoes are imported from Italy. He admits he has a weakness for men's clothing stores and keeps up with the latest fashions, but he doesn't overdo it. He has four pairs of shoes, a handful of suits, and a few dozen shirts and slacks. But he looks so good in them! Jerry has had several problems with women in and out of his parish approaching him, trying to tempt him. Texas is a big state and the women can be quite assertive. But Jerry has an advantage: he is not attracted to them. He loves his vocation, he loves teaching at the private Catholic school next door, and he wouldn't do anything to endanger his "great life," as he puts it. He's never fallen for anything like it.

Andy works on the east coast. He is from a very wealthy family who was disappointed to hear of his career choice: he could have been a vice president in his father's business, but it wasn't even tempting to him. Andy truly enjoys his job as associate pastor in charge of education and youth. He is generous: he gives half of his salary back to the parish and is a self-proclaimed "sucker" for anything the youth are selling at church. He has bought more candy bars, gift wrap, and candles than he'll ever need. But he loves the young people so much and wants to support them. He also enjoys giving his things away.

Andy is in his fourth call and has a peculiar habit. When he leaves a call, he gives everything away except for his books and a minimum of clothing. He depends on the next call to take care of his needs, or he will do without. He is a minimalist and cares about having only the essentials in life. He doesn't like knickknacks, doesn't have shelves of mementos, and his walls are pretty much bare. He likes it that way. He explained to me that it's not that he is making a twisted statement in rejecting his family's lifestyle (as he has been accused of), but it is more his way of adhering to his vow of poverty. He wants to have that tension at the beginning of a call to see what the church will do and how they will take care of him. He feels it gives them an opportunity to set the tone of his tenure there. He also feels it reminds them that he is there to serve them.

Three friends, three vows. Ron, Jerry, and Andy love being priests. They thoroughly enjoy the blessings the priestly life gives them, although they are quick to add that they are never shocked at anything anyone says in confession. They swear they have "heard it all!" And they enjoy the freedom they have to get up and travel, study, and visit with friends. In the Roman Catholic church, the shortage of pastors is severe: there are about seven openings for every available priest, and many churches have to share a priest. But Ron, Jerry, and Andy are at least three who enjoy what they do and are committed to being the best they can be — without women, in obedience, and without excess.

Cuts That Heal

---

*" 'Do not think that I have come to bring peace to the
earth; I have not come to bring peace, but a sword.' "
(v. 34)*

Sally was excited to see her uncle again. Uncle Patrick was a
medical student and he had been away at school in London, England, for five years. She remembered him when she last saw him.
She had only been seven years old, but Uncle Patrick had played
dollies with her, and he had given her bubble gum. Sally was an
only child, and she had loved the attention. She had loved the chance
to play, too, even though he had come to visit her parents. How
eager she was to see him again!

Her mom was beside herself with joy. Uncle Patrick was her
youngest brother and her favorite. They were very close and talked
on the phone often. A big homecoming party was planned for the
weekend.

They waited at the airport and finally Uncle Patrick walked up
to them with open arms. He gave Sally and her parents a big hug.
He slipped Sally a pack of bubble gum and pinched her freckled
cheek. She wasn't a little girl anymore: she was twelve now. If he
didn't watch out, she might grow to be as tall as her uncle! She was
getting to be a little lady, he said, as he put his arm around her. He
handed her a CD: the latest out from London of her favorite singing group.

Uncle Patrick told all them about London and the sights around
his town. He told Sally all about the museums, the art galleries, the
shops, and the outdoor cafes. He told her about the fog, the homes,
and the medical school. He told her about the outlying rural areas
and the downtown London events. He loved traveling around Europe and living in England, but he was glad to settle down "back

home" and start practicing medicine. He was going to be a resident at a teaching hospital.

Sally was fascinated. She wanted to know all about it and sat in the back of the van with him. Was he going to be a pediatrician and work with children? Was he going to be a plastic surgeon and fix people's scars? Was he going to be an orthopaedist and fix broken bones? It all sounded so important! And think of all the money he would make!

Patrick shook his head and roared with laughter. He swore he would make enough money to keep buying Sally CDs, but he told her that there was such a thing as student loans. He was going to be paying those back for many, many years to come.

Sally wanted to know what kind of doctor Uncle Patrick was going to be, and when he told her he was going to be a surgeon, she was very disappointed. She didn't like his choice and suggested he try something else, but Uncle Patrick only laughed. This made Sally all the more serious in her argument. A surgeon cuts into people. A surgeon cuts things out. A surgeon's work is very bloody, she informed him.

Uncle Patrick agreed. It could get quite bloody, he said, but a skilled surgeon has to cut into a person to get to the problem. A surgeon has to cut something out before a person can really be healed.

He told Sally about a man who had had a heart attack when he was only 33. His father had had a serious heart attack too and died at the age of forty. This man was frightened: he didn't want to die at an early age. Uncle Patrick was on the team to observe the surgery, and they found that a blood vessel was constricted. It was corrected with surgery. The surgery was bloody, it was long, and it had to be done exactly right. When the man woke up from surgery, he was told his heart had been repaired and he could expect to live a long time. The man was so grateful for the surgery!

Uncle Patrick told Sally about the little girl whose hand was lost in a grain auger in the outskirts of London. She was only three years old. Friends had found the hand and they were able to reattach it. Patrick had watched the reattachment and had been there for two of the follow-up surgeries. It was an ugly surgery when the hand was attached. The little girl would have to have lots of physical therapy, but the hand should work well enough not to call attention to itself.

Uncle Patrick had watched the plastic surgeon do a fine job of making the scars much smaller on the little girl's hand. He had pulled the jagged edges into a long, thin line, and it appeared as a crease in her arm instead of an ugly cut. The little girl would probably not remember the accident, and her arm should heal enough to have only small lines on it.

Such delicate, meticulous work was what Uncle Patrick wanted to do. He loved the idea of being able to repair things and give people a chance for a healthier life. He wanted to help people get better. But first he would have to cut into them and cut things out. His cuts would heal them, he assured her.

Growing Up — It's A Scary Thought

" 'Whoever welcomes you welcomes me, and whoever welcomes me welcomes the one who sent me. Whoever welcomes a prophet in the name of a prophet will receive a prophet's reward; and whoever welcomes a righteous person in the name of a righteous person will receive the reward of the righteous; and whoever gives even a cup of cold water to one of these little ones in the name of a disciple — truly I tell you, none of these will lose their reward.' " (vv. 40-42)

My parents sacrificed so that my sister and I could go to college. At that time, I mistakenly took it for granted that every college student had a gasoline credit card. I figured everyone had been given a reliable, used car to get around. I thought every college student's "job" was "school." I couldn't imagine an outside job beside all that studying and reading.

Boy, was my thinking ever impaired! Was I ever ignorant! I was so wrong! I must have had my head in the sand for seventeen years. My eyes were opened to reality in college.

My friend, Karen, had worked two jobs at fast food restaurants during high school to be able to buy a car to get to college. She lived forty miles away and she had to pay for her own gas and car insurance. Yet I didn't think twice about hopping in her car to go to the burger place down the street.

Another friend, Glenn, went to school full-time so he could get a scholarship. But he also had to work thirty hours a week. He needed the benefits the grocery store offered because, after his dad's death, his mother's insurance only covered her and his younger sisters. Glenn was too old to be covered anymore. He was nineteen.

Chrissy had a hard life. One could tell just by looking at that serious expression. She looked at everyone as if she were challenging them to a fight. She was an intense kind of gal. Chrissy, it turned out, was a single mother of little twin girls who went to the college's day care. She worked at night at the bank, cleaning the carpets and desks, so that she could afford her books, day care, and a car. She had a heart of gold, but it took me a while to get past that feisty expression before I could see it.

Karen, Glenn, and Chrissy were more normal that I thought. As I got along further and further in school, I realized what a privilege it was to be handed a credit card and told to buy books and supplies as I needed them. It was never questioned. I didn't take advantage of it: I bought my books and gave my dad the receipt. All nicely taken care of. No sweat on my part. A big sacrifice, I realize now, on my mom and dad's part.

They worked hard so my sister and I could get through college. And after college, we were expected to go out into the world and do good, be good, and expect good from others.

My sister, Ingrid, has been teaching for 22 years. I envy her. She knew what she wanted after her second year of college, went for it, and stuck with it. She's on her way to being a school administrator. She is respected for her hard work, and she's known for her tough, yet fair, manner with her elementary students. How many lives has she touched through her efforts? How many children has she inspired to do their best?

About six years after my sister started teaching, she began to receive graduation announcements. Young people came back to see her often at their old elementary school. She was touched to be able to go to graduations, weddings, and other celebrations. But she has also gone to funerals, court trials, and the hospital with her former students. She has seen teens have babies, teens commit suicide, and teens kill others. It's a cruel world sometimes, but Ingrid loves the children.

They know it. They can feel it. They can see it in everything she does.

My mom and dad sacrificed so we could be prepared to go out into the world and do good. As the prophet in the passage was told, so Ingrid and I were told to welcome others and welcome the one who sent them. And we have been welcomed in return. We have been given a cup of cold water and welcomed by righteous people.

Be good. Do good. Expect others to do good also.

Proper 9/Ordinary Time 14
Matthew 11:16-19, 25-30

"Jesus Is Not In A Shed, Mom!"

"At that time Jesus said, 'I thank you, Father, Lord of heaven and earth, because you have hidden these things from the wise and the intelligent and have revealed them to infants; yes, Father, for such was your gracious will.' " (vv. 25-26)

I — along with other parents around the world — have learned so much about faith from the casual comments of my children. Their innocence is refreshing. Their easy style of believing without seeing is a great example. Their sincere faith is a testimony to others at times.

Our son, Andrew, always says whatever the pastor says at the altar. No matter if it is the greeting, the liturgy, the words of institution, or the blessing, my Andrew mumbles along quietly with the pastor. I didn't think it was so odd because their father is a pastor, and they have been to more than a few church services in their lives. Our daughter, Kjrstin, also "talks" along with the pastor — even at ten years of age. It sounds like they are whispering.

One Sunday, we needed to get away. Actually, my husband, a hospital chaplain, needed to get away. Ten of his oncology and critical care patients had died that week, and he was finding it hard to be pastoral. He was weary, he was sad, and he was getting melancholy. We decided to visit friends for the weekend.

We were invited to their church and were told we could choose from four services. They preferred the contemporary service and asked if we were interested. It was an upbeat service, Bill said, consisting of a band of thirty youth, lots of songs projected on a huge screen, and just a tiny sermon. Andrew thought it sounded cool. Kjrstin thought it sounded like a great idea.

The church was packed: 450 of us sitting on comfortable, padded chairs lined up in rows, facing a stage. A large group of young people were playing guitars, drums, and flutes and holding microphones. One boy was playing the violin, and another was shaking a tambourine. My children were truly attentive because they didn't know what was coming. The songs were very familiar, and there was much enthusiasm in the air during the service.

Our friend, Bill, one of six pastors at the church, led the service. He gave a little pep talk, we sang a lot, and we were sent away "to be a blessing to the world."

After church, back at the house, the adults sat around and talked and laughed and shared much with each other. The children were playing games downstairs, and it was an enjoyable afternoon. Soon, we were on our way home.

We asked our children what they thought of the service, and they both thought it was "cool." They liked the instruments (Kjrstin plays the viola and was very interested in the string section). Andrew liked the guitar player's "way cool" colorful strap. Kjrstin liked the girls singing up front.

The ride was over an hour long and soon the children were reading and playing and things quieted down. As my husband slept on the seat beside me, I glanced back at Kjrstin, who was reading her book. Andrew seemed to be talking to himself. I focused in on what he was saying. "The body of Christ, given for you. The blood of Christ, shared for you." He was playing with a Max Steel mountain climber, who was seated at the edge of his chair, holding a doll-sized cup in his hand. "The blood of Christ, shared for you," Andrew said.

"Hey, honey, did you say *shared*? Or *shed*?" I don't know why I had to interrupt his thoughts, but I was curious.

Andrew looked up at me. "It's shared, Mom. Jesus shared his blood."

"Honey, I think the word is *shed*, not *shared*. Could that be?"

Andrew laughed and looked at me with his big blue eyes. "Mom, you're so silly! Jesus isn't in a shed! Jesus died on the cross and shared his blood and went to heaven to be with God. That's how Jesus can live in your heart. Mommy, you're too funny!"

Well, okay. I had to think about it for a second. Andrew was dead serious and he turned back to his Max Steel. "The blood of Christ shared for you." He pulled out the rope and attached it to the back of his sister's seat.

Max Steel was going to climb a big mountain.

Mommy was going to forever hear the words of institution in a new light.

Will It Bear Fruit?

---

*" 'But as for what was sown on good soil, this is the
one who hears the word and understands it, who indeed bears fruit and yields, in one case a hundredfold,
in another sixty, and in another thirty.' " (v. 23)*

Melinda's heart ached. Her seventeen-year-old daughter had
just gotten her nose pierced. Marcy wasn't even old enough to go
to college, yet she was old enough to choose to have her nose
pierced. What was to become of her? Melinda hoped this didn't
signal a downward spiral to Marcy's future.

Melinda and Dan faced a big decision. Should they be honest
and share their disappointment, and then end up seeing what other
parts of Marcy's body she could pierce? Would people be quick to
judge her? Or, worse yet, would people not be able to believe she
was a "good Christian girl"? Should they confront her? Or should
they choose their battles, and succinctly state that they were disappointed, and leave it at that?

They took the easy way out — and said nothing. When Marcy
came to the dinner table that night, her little brother told her she
looked silly with her red nose and matching red stone. "The swelling will go down, you goofball." She looked at her parents, but
Melinda and Dan didn't say anything. They just glanced at her
nose and then went on with their conversation. They were trying to
decide which colleges they could visit with Marcy the following
month. What did Marcy want, they asked her. School was out for
three days, and Dan and Melinda wanted to make the most of it.

Marcy had good grades, pulling a solid B average, and was
offered several small scholarships. They had narrowed the choice
to three each: Melinda's three college choices, Dan's three, and
Marcy's three. They weren't allowed to show each other their

choices until later. Each had written down 25 strengths that Marcy had, then they would compare them with each school's academic strengths. Dan secretly wished Marcy would go to his old school: Central Lutheran. Melinda had gone there one year and then went off to graduate at State University. They had been quick to exclude any school focusing on the sciences, Marcy's least favorite subjects. Whatever the college, they hoped Marcy would love it and have a positive experience.

They had rented a fancy hotel suite for the weekend, and the family lounged around and talked about Marcy's goals in life, and they divulged their choices to each other. Melinda was a little anxious; Dan was very anxious. Marcy seemed to enjoy the excitement.

Two college names came up: Northwestern and State College. Not exactly Dan and Melinda's first choices, but they had also considered the schools for their strong liberal arts backgrounds. They prayed about it as a family and told Marcy they would discuss it and pray about it for an entire month and then let Marcy decide. Marcy ended up going to Northwestern.

Dan and Melinda were nervous wrecks that first week of college. They were constantly calling Marcy only to hang up the phone before it rang. They didn't want to be so obvious. They missed her terribly and stuck to the promised Wednesday and Sunday calls.

They were ecstatic when Marcy's first holiday break allowed her to be home for three weeks. They noticed she had an earring on her upper right earlobe. They didn't say anything. They wanted this to be a positive homecoming. They were so happy to hear about her experiences: it was so much richer than hearing it over the phone!

Marcy's college experience was positive: she met wonderful friends. She also made a deeper commitment to God. One night, she waited until her little brother was in bed before she called her parents into her bedroom to share her story. She was excited!

In a Bible study in the dorm one afternoon soon after college started, Marcy shared her frustration about being a "good Christian girl." A young man challenged her. He was a senior and he was a little brash. He told her being from a strong Christian family didn't qualify her as being a "good Christian girl". He wanted to know just what she meant by that anyway. Did that mean she was good at *being Christian*? Or was Marcy good because she *was* a Christian? What did she do to show her faith anyway?

Marcy was insulted and taken aback by the boy's frankness. The group had a good discussion, some siding with Marcy, some egging the boy on. In the end the boy shared that he was from a "good Christian home," too, but it wasn't until he was challenged to show good Christian actions that he felt called to have a closer relationship with Christ. It was the turning point he needed in his life. He went on to give his testimony of faith. One night in his freshman year, the boy was praying as he always did: a little quickly, a little distractedly, when he felt he needed to pray really in earnest. He asked God sincerely for direction in his life, and over the course of that week he got an answer: he wanted to teach anyway, but now his direction was for children in urban, secular schools where they needed a good role model. He shared that that conviction lead him to change his focus of study and lifestyle, and he became a minimalist, one who lives with as few possessions as possible in order to give generously to others.

"And you think," Marcy asked, "that just by teaching poor kids that *you* are going to be a better Christian?" Marcy couldn't believe his arrogance! "No," the boy said. "I believe that if I go back to my neighborhood, the kids — who know me already — will listen to me and will understand that if I can get out of such a poor neighborhood, they can too. I can share my struggles with them both with school and with having to resist gangs and drugs every day. And I can give them hope to be somebody. I didn't think I'd live to be fourteen. And then when I did, I thought I wouldn't make it to sixteen. I figured I would have been shot by then for resisting gangs or maybe I would be slipped some dangerous drugs. But with God's help, I was able to avoid it, and I went to school. I played my music, got a good scholarship, and did my best in school. If I can do it, they surely can do it! They just need God's direction like I needed it in my freshman year."

Wow! What a speech. The group was touched by his bravery in sharing his story. Marcy was eternally sorry that she thought he was arrogant. He just didn't "look" like a poor kid. "I'm very sorry," she mumbled.

"Ah, but looks are deceiving, aren't they?" he said. He lifted up his shirt sleeve to reveal an ugly tattoo of a dragon sucking on a skull. It went all the way up his arm. He lifted up his pant leg to reveal a tiger tattooed around his leg, eating what looked like a dead body. "I can never swim again without being hastily judged by these two creatures on my body. But what's inside of me — in my very being — is harder to guess. I like to call it a pleasant surprise."

Marcy was breathless when she shared this with her parents. "Wow! Can you believe it?" She kissed them both and went to bed, leaving them speechless. It was only the first of many times she shared with them what she was experiencing at college.

Marcy graduated with a degree in art history and works as a manager in a small art gallery. Her husband is a very successful diesel-engine mechanic. They have small twin boys. They are secure in their careers, and they are secure in their dedication to their faith, teaching Bible school and new adult Christians. They are also minimalists who give fifty percent of their earnings to a mission church. Because of their faith and generosity, two churches have been started from their home church. And because of their faith and generosity in sharing their life journeys, many, many people have come to know Christ in a personal way. They don't think they are better than anyone. They don't brag or belittle anyone. They simply share their faith journey.

And the boy with the tattoos? Well, Marcy still teases her husband's brother for being so forward that day, but that night led her to a closer relationship with Christ — and her future husband.

Bitterness Will Get You Nowhere

---

*" 'Let both of them grow together until the harvest;
and at harvest time I will tell the reapers, Collect the
weeds first and bind them in bundles to be burned, but
gather the wheat into my barn.' " (v. 30)*

Some people cannot communicate unless they are complaining. It's irritating, isn't it? Usually this costs a person friends. Sometimes it may even cost a person his job ...

Greg was forever grumbling. "There's no coffee." "That department has a pizza party and we don't ever get anything fun." "Those warehouse employees get to wear jeans; I have to wear dress pants!" Grumble, grumble, grumble was all Greg did. I secretly called him Grouchy Greg when I shared his latest complaints with my husband.

Greg was a great worker. He was always polite with the customers, helping them find the right part or suggesting tools be used in a different way so they could get more use from them. He was an expert electrician and was very sought after to help neighbors begin electrical projects. But his grumbling alienated him from his co-workers and friends.

Grouchy Greg was busy complaining to a supervisor about the coffee stain on the carpet in front of the break room when he experienced chest pains. We figured he must have been acting because he was so upset and animated about the coffee stain. But Greg's face became white, and he clutched at his left shoulder. He stopped speaking mid-sentence and looked strange. The supervisor immediately called 911 from his cell phone and had Greg sit down. We were all concerned and the paramedics had to fight a small crowd when they came to take Greg to the hospital several minutes later.

We were all so worried! I have to say I felt terribly guilty over past ungracious thoughts of Greg as I asked God to spare his life.

It was over six months before Greg could return to work. More workers had been added in his department, he didn't remember the prices that well anymore, but everyone was patient and understanding during his transition. He was back to his old level of giving excellent advice in no time. And in no time he was back to his grumbling.

Greg's manager was promoted to supervisor in another department. Greg had just a little more experience, and Greg and one other co-worker were interviewed for the manager's position. They each had positive interviews, and it came down to the senior manager to make the final decision.

"You both have had the same opportunities, the same conditions, and the same level of training. I've decided to promote Nancy because of her positive outlook for the company. She is upbeat when speaking about the company, she never complains about her colleagues, and she has a positive approach to her work. Nancy will be the new manager."

Greg grumbled louder than ever the following days. He moaned that it was all unfair, it was surely because of his heart attack, or it was a sexist issue. The manager called Greg in.

"Make no mistake about this, Greg. You give the best advice to our customers because of your electrician background. But you were passed over because you complain, whine, and whimper about any little thing. Instead of suggesting a remedy, you continue to whine until you find something else to complain about. It's unproductive, irritating, and, frankly, it has come between you and a promotion. I hope you give it careful thought."

Greg's head hung low as he slithered out of the office. He thought about it. He had a pre-existing condition as far as his insurance coverage was concerned and, at 56, was not likely going to find another good job so easily. He did like his job. He would have to learn to adjust. And maybe he would have to learn to adjust his attitude. Just a little bit.

It was Greg's brother who helped adjust Greg's attitude. "Every time you think you need to be a grouch, write a note about something that's good. Look at the bright side and stop being such a pain in the patooty! Man, you can be quite a headache!"

It took years to turn Greg's grumpiness into gratitude. But as more and more positive things came to light, less and less negative things surfaced. Greg took to writing little notes and sticking them in surprising little places for people to find: in calendars, on a locker, on the window of a car. He wrote little notes to his co-workers when he saw good things happen. He wrote the punch lines of jokes he had shared earlier in the day. And he wrote thank you notes to the janitors for their efforts.

Grumpy Greg never made it to manager of his department, but he made quite an impression on his supervisor when he was asked to take charge of the new trainees: the "newbies." He was chosen for his positive attitude. After all, enthusiasm is contagious!

Extraordinary Ordinary Things

"He put before them another parable: 'The kingdom of heaven is like a mustard seed that someone took and sowed in his field; it is the smallest of all the seeds, but when it has grown it is the greatest of shrubs and becomes a tree, so that the birds of the air come and make nests in its branches.' He told them another parable: 'The kingdom of heaven is like yeast that a woman took and mixed in with three measures of flour until all of it was leavened.' " (vv. 31-33)

Catchy quotes help us envision things that are hard to understand. To quote a television preacher: "When you see a seed, envision an apple; when you see an apple, envision an orchard." And "bloom where you are planted." Ordinary images, extraordinary realities.

A tree is quite ordinary. The action of a seed bearing fruit is quite extraordinary. A loaf of bread is quite ordinary. The action of yeast raising the dough is quite mysterious. Jesus used the imagery of ordinary things to explain extraordinary things. Mysterious things.

A seed can be tiny but, with time, it is able to yield a tall, strong tree. The tree grows up to be strong enough to withstand wind and rain. The tree can have many uses, including such important ones as providing shade and giving protection to birds. And all this from a seed. Such big action from a tiny thing! Such big results from a simple act of putting the seed in the ground.

What if we saw the love of God through baptism as the tiny seed within us? The gift of baptism into God's family is no small thing. What if God's love so filled us that we were able to yield a strong faith? A faith so strong that it can get us through life's normal ups and downs — as well as times of great stress or trauma. A faith so strong that when faced with adversity, we can still turn to God for strength and comfort. A faith so strong that God can sustain us when no one or nothing else can.

A loaf of bread is made with common ingredients: salt, flour, water, yeast. The bread is raised as the yeast literally explodes through a chemical action. An amazing process takes place inside such an ordinary thing as a loaf of bread.

What would happen if we saw the Word of God as yeast in our lives? Something so ordinary as words are extraordinary when read in the Scriptures. Ordinary words; extraordinary meanings. When we place God's words deep in our hearts they sustain us through tough times. When we keep the meaning of these words in our minds, there is little room for negative, destructive, or unfaithful thoughts. When we put these words into meaning in our lives, we live lives according to God's will. Such an ordinary thing as words can bear such fruit in our lives!

Jesus used ordinary things to describe the kingdom of heaven. We can use ordinary events such as reading Scriptures and remembering our baptism to have a deeper faith life. Ordinary things can turn a person's life into an extraordinary vessel to be used by God.

Attending To The Needs Of Others First

"Now when Jesus heard this, he withdrew from there in a boat to a deserted place by himself. But when the crowds heard it, they followed him on foot from the towns. When he went ashore, he saw a great crowd; and he had compassion for them and cured their sick. When it was evening, the disciples came to him and said, 'This is a deserted place, and the hour is now late; send the crowds away so that they may go into the villages and buy food for themselves.' Jesus said to them, 'They need not go away; you give them something to eat.' " (vv. 13-16)

John was tired. He could hardly stand up. He needed rest. Mrs. Ho's surgery had been very intense and, although the team was great, he felt it his responsibility to stay with the woman until her vital signs strengthened. He wanted to be close, but he needed to rest. He called the charge nurse, instructing Shirley to keep someone close to Mrs. Ho and let him know if there was any change at all in her vital signs. He would be asleep in the doctors' lounge down the hall. The lounge was probably deserted at this early hour in the morning, and he desperately needed to nap and catch a quick bite. He counted the change in his pocket. He wolfed down a granola bar, gulped a pint of milk, and fell asleep instantly on a couch in the corner.

John had slept 28 minutes when the charge nurse beeped him. His training didn't fail him: he sat up, called the number, and was instantly attuned to what Shirley was saying. Mrs. Ho's blood pressure was dropping. John was on his way and in the room in record time. He attended to Mrs. Ho, waited with her, and gave instructions to the nurse. Two hours later, Mrs. Ho's vitals appeared to turn around, and John felt himself relax. He also felt intense fatigue. He needed to rest.

He headed back to the lounge, and this time it was busy with doctors chatting and snacking, waiting to start their morning rounds. It was six o'clock in the morning. John stumbled to the corner couch, faced the wall and put his jacket over his head. He fell into a deep sleep. He slept soundly for two hours until he was beeped. Eight o'clock in the morning! He wanted to start rounds, but he needed to check on Mrs. Ho and the two others he had operated on yesterday. But an emergency was coming in and they would have to wait. He needed to focus on the car accident victim coming in.

The victim had a broken leg and lots of bleeding on her face from superficial cuts, but nothing was bleeding internally. John was thankful. He patched up the young girl, told her to slow down on those slick gravel roads, and told her she'd be as good as new in no time. Her cuts were along the eyebrow and hairline. She wouldn't know they had been there after a few months. John was pleased for the girl; she was pretty.

He called the charge nurse up on third. Mrs. Ho was sleeping comfortably and was responding to the IV he had given her earlier. She was coming along nicely. John headed up to sixth to check on the others who had had surgery yesterday. Mr. Ortega looked good: his color had returned to his face and his pulse and blood pressure were very strong. John was delighted. John smiled broadly into the phone as he told the patient's wife that Mr. Ortega should be ready to go home in about a week.

Wendy was another story. She had been a difficult case, and the surgery was very intricate. John had been satisfied with the procedure although Wendy wasn't as stable as he wanted. He was curious about her progress as he headed to her room, but he was interrupted by another beep. A level-one trauma was coming in on the air ambulance in thirteen minutes. John called the shift nurse and asked how Wendy was. Wendy wasn't doing so well, but Dr. Carter had been in to see her. John gave some instructions and told them he'd be there to see her as soon as he was finished with the boy being flown in. He asked the nurse to keep Dr. Carter abreast of any change and to beep Dr. Carter should the need arise. John was needed in the emergency room. He was on full-alert.

The boy came in with several problems: a broken wrist and arm and a cracked shoulder. His leg had been twisted out of its socket, and there were several cuts to his back. The boy had been involved in an early morning tractor roll-over. John felt sorry for the boy as he cried out in pain. For over an hour John worked diligently on the boy and was satisfied with the osteopath's assessments. The orthopaedist was also working on the boy, and things would settle down shortly. Seeing everything was under control, John went to tell the boy's family the good news. They could see him in about twenty minutes.

John was tired. He needed to sleep. But first he wanted to check on Wendy. He headed up the stairs, but Dr. Carter met him in the stairwell. Wendy had died, and Dr. Carter and the chaplain had already talked to the family. John felt sad as he headed for the door.

He filled out papers for an hour, charting his actions and instructions. He got his coat and started for home. He was off call twenty minutes ago. He would rest. There was so much to be done. So much that needed his and others' constant attention. But he also needed to take care of himself. He needed rest so that he could continue to be helpful.

A Rough Ride

---

*"But immediately Jesus spoke to them and said, 'Take
heart, it is I; do not be afraid.' " (v. 27)*

Gail, a fourth year graduate student, asked the first year women
if they wanted to go for a boat ride on Saturday. Carol, Bonnie,
Krista, Cindy, and Debbie were just starting graduate school. Gail
had been their tour guide on the first day of classes, and they had
struck up a good conversation. Gail had showed them where everything was: the dining hall, the campus mail center, the state-of-
the-art library, the student lounges strategically placed throughout
the campus, and several other necessary offices and buildings they
would need to be familiar with in the course of their schooling.

They saw each other often on the small campus, and the group
was looking forward to the trip to the lake. Lake Murray was twenty
miles away, set in the midst of rolling hills and surrounded by thick
trees. It was a hot summer day and the boat ride would be a wonderful treat. They headed out at about ten in the morning, eagerly
anticipating a relaxing day. The sky was cloudless.

Gail's van pulled the boat effortlessly down the highway toward the lake. When they arrived, Gail checked various things at
the lake while the others threw towels, sunscreen, and snacks onto
the boat. Cindy laughingly tweaked the emergency horn, which
squealed loudly. Boaters nearby yelled hi, and Gail apologized to
them. She explained to Cindy that the horn was only to be used in
an absolute emergency, since any nearby boaters would feel obli-
gated to go out and assist a stranded boat.

Krista was from Minnesota and had grown up on a lake. She
expertly helped Gail unhook the boat from the hitch, pull in the
ropes, and get the boat into the water. The girls laughed as they

jumped in. It was a beautiful day, and Gail was surprised to see so few boats out.

Gail raced across the lake, showing them what the boat could do. Carol was from North Carolina. She admitted she was afraid of water, but she sat on the bottom of the boat by Krista's feet and was okay with the speed. Bonnie, who was from Nevada, loved speed and sat right up front with Gail, letting her long curly hair flap in the wind. It felt good to have the spray of water hitting her face! Cindy and Debbie were too busy chatting to notice anything. On their first day tour with Gail, they had discovered they were from the same big city in Texas, and today they were comparing notes. They hadn't known each other, but it turned out they had some friends in common.

On the quiet lake, Gail slowed to a crawl, pointing out different lake homes and cabins along the waterfront. She pointed out a century-old home that had been Lake Murray's first permanent lake home. She told them about her tour through the home several Christmases ago, recalling how beautifully it had been decorated for the holidays. There were many interesting houses to be seen on the shore. It was a lovely boat ride.

Gail anchored close to shore in a cove. She joked that the water snakes would like the girls' suntan lotion and finally convinced Debbie that she was actually kidding. The snakes were on the other side of the lake! The six of them floated on inner tubes, swam, and chatted in the water until Carol mentioned she was getting cold. Gail looked up at the sky and thought it was getting awfully dark to the south. The wind had picked up, and she suggested they eat their picnic lunch in the boat while she headed toward the other side of the lake and the dock. The weather could change at a second's notice. Lake Murray is a very long lake and they had quite a long way to go. Gail didn't mention anything aloud, but the sky looked very strange. She was quiet as they started back.

The girls were eating their picnic lunch when Cindy asked why the sky was turning orange. It looked eerie. Krista was very alarmed; there were no boats on the lake as far as they could see. Gail stepped on the accelerator, anxious to hurry back. Suddenly, there was a loud bang as thunder clapped overhead. Cindy swore it was right over their boat, and Gail yelled for them to get the blankets out from under the seats. She made sure their life vests were snapped tightly around them. It started to rain. Gail was clearly worried.

Gail gunned the engine only to hear it die. She tried to start it, but there was no response. Krista gave it a try but was worried it would flood. The boat was being blown back toward the cove. They were all clearly worried as another clap of thunder hit overhead. It started to pour. Gail was beside herself as she watched Carol scream. Carol was hysterical. Krista and Cindy pulled Carol close to them and covered her with blankets that were drenched. Carol curled up in a ball on the boat floor and covered her ears. She was crying loudly.

Bonnie was confused and worried. Why would the engine die? And what should they do? She had no idea until Krista pulled the airhorn from the glove compartment. She sounded it slowly four times, once pointed toward the north, then toward the south, east, and west. Gail nodded her head in approval and tried the engine again. Her cell phone was dead, and they would either have to get the engine going or wait for help. Gail looked out over the water. Not one boat was on the water. Krista sounded the air horn again, slowly and deliberately pointing it in all directions. The girls prayed hard, knowing their only hope was to wait for help.

Carol, Bonnie, Krista, Cindy, Debbie, and Gail were sitting in the boat on Lake Murray wondering what to do, when through the pouring rain a pontoon boat appeared. An elderly couple was on board and they called out to the girls. "Are you okay? Do you need help?" The girls looked through the rain — they weren't seeing ghosts. An older couple was offering them help. Welcome help!

Gail efficiently tied the boat to the pontoon and jumped on board. She would guide the pontoon; Krista would guide the boat. Carol was escorted onto the covered pontoon, seated between the couple. She quieted down in a hurry, relieved to be with the kindly woman and man. The couple said they had noticed the girls a few hours earlier as they were swimming in the cove. They lived just to the west and had remarked that the girls were quite brave to ignore the weather warnings broadcast on the radio. When the couple heard the emergency horn, they assumed the girls hadn't heard the radio and decided to check it out. Actually, they weren't that far from shore. Gail thanked the couple over and over again and started to cry. She felt responsible for the girls, and she hadn't known severe weather was on the way. She felt as if she had failed them.

The group made it to shore in a few minutes. Gail was able to tie the pontoon at the couple's dock with her boat tied to the other side. She threw on the canvas cover as they all dashed up to the couple's cabin. It was such a relief to be safe and inside! The group thanked the couple profusely.

The man had been quiet the whole time. He held up his hand. "You have to thank the missus. I was going to go to town today, but the missus thought we should stay, even though bad weather was on the way. She said in her morning devotions she had the feeling she should stay at our cabin today. I thought she was a little crazy, but you don't argue with the missus when she says something like that. We've been living here for 32 summers, you know. I got my cards out and we stayed. We were playing cards when we saw you girls going to the cove. The grandkids love that place too. The weather turned so quickly, and we were relieved to see you head out. Then it started raining so fast we couldn't see you. We wouldn't have heard your horn, but the missus was standing in the sun porch looking to see if she could still see you folks. She was sure she heard a horn, and then a few minutes later heard it again, and she yelled for me to come. I never heard it, but the missus has good ears. So we thought you couldn't be too far, and we got on the pontoon. It was kind of a bumpy ride, you know. I don't think I want to do that again!"

No, neither did the girls as they spent the rest of the afternoon playing cards and drying their clothes. The couple served them leftover soup, and the mood turned festive when the rain finally ended. It had been a rough day, but God had been with them. God had sent them these kinds folks. God had not foresaken them in the midst of Lake Murray.

Oh, To Be Quiet!

---

*"Then he called the crowd to him and said to them,
'Listen and understand: it is not what goes into the
mouth that defiles a person, but it is what comes out of
the mouth that defiles.' " (vv. 10-11)*

Lucy had a big mouth. Not literally, for she had a beautiful
mouth. But her lips were moving constantly, either because she
was chewing gum or talking. She talked incessantly. Lucy was very
rough. She told funny stories, sometimes with innuendo and sometimes outright crass.

Lucy could be very rude and her mouth was definitely her down-
fall. As a teen, she had applied for a job, and during the interview
she mentioned she thought the woman's blouse was not her best
color. Lucy understandably was not hired. She was a whiz at math,
and when she applied for an entry-level bookkeeping job, Lucy
made the mistake of telling the lady she intended to move up the
ladder and be promoted in record time. The lady didn't really take
kindly to Lucy's cocky attitude.

Lucy found a job as an accounting clerk, and she did climb up
the ladder quickly, especially once she became a certified public
accountant. Lucy loved her job and was good with numbers, but
she wasn't so good with people. She talked while she worked, even
though her work was excellent. She couldn't stop talking!

Lucy ordered people around at work. She was rude to the
checker who didn't ring up an order fast enough. She often tipped
one penny to show her dissatisfaction. Lucy was becoming a leg-
end in eateries around the business district. Many waiters or waitresses either ignored her completely or exaggerated their care of
her. Either way, they were usually tipped one penny as she recounted
all their mistakes.

Nan didn't know Lucy. Nan had just moved from New York. She was very excited about her husband's fantastic job, and she felt fortunate that the restaurant owner let her work from 9 a.m. to 2 p.m. so Nan could be home for their two daughters. But she was homesick for the hustle and bustle of New York: Nan liked the energy and excitement. But she was determined to make a new home here, find friends in their new church, and make the best of it. She was very outgoing, was not afraid to say what she thought, and was very kind. That's why Nan loved waitressing. It was hard work, but she loved talking and listening to people, and she liked the demand of remembering the orders and the particular tastes of the regular customers and getting things on the tables on time. She was a very good waitress, if she did say so herself. And her boss said so, too. He could see it by the way she looked around the restaurant before her interview. She had picked up a dirty glass from the table next door and put it on the counter to be noticed. He loved Nan right away.

It was inevitable that Nan and Lucy would meet. Lucy walked in one day, and the waitress came running to the back. She told Nan she would take her break, and Nan could cover the two tables at the front. Lucy was sitting at one table by herself. A piece of cake, Nan thought, until she got closer and saw Lucy frown. "Hello! Anything in particular I can get you? Our specials today are turkey noodle soup, ham on rye, and chocolate silk pie. May I take your order, or would you like to look at the menu for a bit?"

Lucy looked up at Nan and slowly looked her over — top to bottom. She smirked. Nan wasn't intimidated. "Well, I'm clean as you can see. Did you want to order yet, or shall I come back?" Nan looked right at Lucy and waited for an answer. Lucy looked back at her and said nothing.

"Well, I have other customers I need to attend to. Please hold up your hand when you are ready to order." With that, Nan was gone in a flash, leaving Lucy with an open mouth. She let Lucy hold her hand up twenty seconds before she came and took her order. Nan wanted to make sure Lucy understood she was not going to be treated like a third-class citizen. Lucy wanted to make sure Nan understood she was going to be treated like a preferred customer.

As expected, Lucy left Nan a penny. Nan kept it, taping it to an index card with notes scribbled on it. Nan left word that the next time Lucy came in, she would personally take Lucy's order. Nan was miffed, having attended to every change that Lucy wanted in her order, and she did not deserve to be treated rudely. The penny didn't matter; the attitude did.

Lucy came in two days later, and Nan was ready. Nan walked right up to her and asked her if she could take her order. Lucy mumbled she wanted the same as last time. But Nan was ready. "No, last time you changed your order three times, and you sent it back after you ate half of it. I don't think we got it quite right because you only left me a penny. Let's get your order, go over it, and make sure we get it right for you. What can I get you?" Lucy stared at Nan. That audacity! The nerve of this woman! Lucy asked for another waitress. "No one else is here, and the owner wants me to personally see that your order is correct. What can I get you?" Nan smiled at Lucy. Lucy mumbled her order. When it came, she wanted something changed, but Nan got out her card. "It is exactly as you ordered it — and, exactly as you ordered it Monday. If you would like to make a new order, that would be fine, but you will be charged. Would you like to make a new order?" Nan smiled.

Lucy looked at Nan, up and down. Nan smiled. Lucy frowned, threw down money, and left. Nan kept the change: 42 cents. She made a note of it on her card. Lucy came in again the following Monday, and Nan was ready for her, making small talk and trying to get Lucy to open up. She felt sorry for Lucy and wanted to know what would have made her such a mean-spirited person. Lucy asked for another waitress. "Well, I have to honestly tell you that no one wants to wait on you. You get to see me every time you walk through the door and want to order something. The others will not tolerate your abuse. The owner is very supportive of this and welcomes you to make an order if you still want to. We like our customers, but we are human and will not take this. May I take your order?" Nan smiled sweetly. Lucy gave her order. She tried to change it, but Nan had her card ready and showed that this was in fact exactly

144

the way Lucy had asked for it. She was welcome to make a new order. Lucy ate her sandwich.

So it went on for several weeks until Nan knew exactly what Lucy wanted and Lucy was actually happy with her order. She never showed it, but she didn't complain. She left her change, which was always under a dollar, but Nan didn't mind. She felt she was getting connected to Lucy.

One day, Nan was on her day off, and she came to the restaurant to pick up her paycheck. She heard Lucy come in and ask for Nan. Nan went over and explained she wasn't working that day, but could they have lunch together? Nan didn't wait for an answer, sat down across from Lucy, and ordered for both Lucy and herself, telling the waitress to write down the order carefully. The nervous waitress brought their sandwiches in record time.

Nan and Lucy talked awkwardly at first, but then Nan got to the guts: Did Lucy hate waitresses? Was she a waitress when she was young and had a bad experience? Why was she so rude? Nan was persistent, yet kind when she asked her why Lucy — a beautiful and obviously educated woman — would treat people so meanly. Nan told her she could see by the way she dressed that she cared for herself, but why didn't she care for others? Lucy looked at Nan for a long time.

It was the first of several lunches for the two women, who started seeing each other outside the restaurant. Nan's husband and children didn't like Lucy, but Nan insisted she come to their home. Eventually, Lucy shared that her father had owned a restaurant, and her mother had to wait tables. Her father was never satisfied with anything her mother or Lucy did and he was very abusive. Her mother finally got up the courage to leave her father and she took Lucy across the state line, only to end up in a women's shelter. Lucy hated her father for being so mean; she hated her mother for making her live for three months in a shelter. But they got on their feet, and Lucy and her mother made a comfortable life for themselves after a while. But Lucy couldn't get over her anger with her father.

Nan knew Bible study was not a cure-all, but she invited Lucy to her Bible study; there was someone there Nan wanted Lucy to know. Lucy refused. But Nan was persistent, and Lucy finally came. She didn't say anything at first, but when a young woman shared that she was trying to save money so she could leave her abusive husband, Lucy was all ears. The young woman showed her bruises, and the women cried with her and for her as they offered their help. Lucy finally spoke up. Lucy told the young woman to get out as soon as she could. She talked about her experience, the hurt, the physical and emotional pain, and the hatred she had for her father. She couldn't help herself; Lucy just kept on talking. Nan held her hand as Lucy shared her story. It helped the young woman; it helped Lucy to get it out.

Lucy went to counseling at Nan's urging, which she is still in after two years. This is a serious issue; it will take time. Lucy came to know the women at the Bible study well and — with time — was able to speak in a gentler way. Lucy will always be known for her "big mouth," but she has been sensitized to the fact that not everything that comes out of her mouth helps others. But now not everything that comes out of her mouth hurts either. Lucy is slowly learning.

Proper 16/Ordinary Time 21
Romans 12:1-8

Conformed Or Transformed?

"Do not be conformed to this world, but be transformed
by the renewing of your minds, so that you may discern
what is the will of God — what is good and acceptable
and perfect." (v. 2)

This little verse packs a lot of punch. It has many words that
are full of meaning, full of insight, full of information about what
God wants for us as a community of God.

Conformed: To be conformed is to mold or form one's behavior in accordance with a particular pattern. Some of us need a certain label on our back pants pocket to feel we're acceptable; others
pierce their bodies to fit in with a certain crowd; still others drive a
particular car to seem worthy. The ideal would be to mold our behavior in accordance to God's pattern.

World: The world in which we live now, not the future or the
past. We live in the world the way it is right now. It may not be the
way we want it to be, but it is the way it is.

Transformed: The root of *transformed* is from the Greek *mete-
morph*, to be changed, changed into, or to become. We recall the
metamorphosis of a caterpillar into a beautiful butterfly. We see
the metamorphosis of an awkward teenager into a composed, confident adult.

Renew: Refreshed, alive again, ready to go on again. We need
periods of renewal so that we can go out into our daily lives, in the
world in which we live, to be the people God wants us to be.

Discern: A discernment is a testing of sorts: an examination, a
discovery, an interpretation. We can discern things when we discover the particulars, when we examine it thoroughly and ask God
for an interpretation.

147

Will of God: God's will is that we be the people we were meant to be, and people who live in peace, act mercifully and justly, and who walk in God's love and light. The will of God is that which would please God.

Good: Would this be moral goodness? Or someone's positive worth? God wants positive aspects in our lives and wants us in turn to bring about positive growth and attitudes.

Acceptable: Something that is pleasing to someone is considered acceptable.

Perfect: Perfection is the ultimate goal. It is complete, truly genuine, and fully accomplished.

So many words, such a little sentence. Paul told the Christian community in Rome that he would be visiting them. Paul did not yet begin or visit the church in Rome, which was started around the year 49-50, but Paul wanted to introduce himself to them since he intended to pass through Rome on his way to Spain. He was asking them to be members — fully participating members — of the people of God.

Paul reminded the members of this new community that they have been given God-given talents, resources, and responsibilities, not only toward one another, but as a church body. They must work together. They must renew their minds so that they can discern and understand the will of God. They must do what is good and acceptable.

Paul told them that if they conform to God's will, they would be transformed in doing God's will. Amen!

Why Does This Have To Happen?

<hr>

*"From that time on, Jesus began to show his disciples
that he must go to Jerusalem and undergo great suffering at the hands of the elders and chief priests and
scribes, and be killed, and on the third day be raised.
And Peter took him aside and began to rebuke him, saying, 'God forbid it, Lord! This must never happen to
you.' " (vv. 21-22)*

Mae is Chris' best friend. Mae would do just about anything
for Chris, who grew up down the street from her. Chris is one year
older, and he had picked on Mae when she moved into the neighborhood. They were standing at the bus stop, and Mae was looking
very nervous. Chris called her a name, feeling very much the smart
first grader. But when Chris saw that Mae was crying, he instantly
regretted it. He came after school that day and apologized, offering
her a race car as a peace offering.

Chris came to Mae's house with his dad. Chris was a gentle
soul; his dad knew Chris had to make amends because Chris
wouldn't stop talking about making the new girl cry; he was very
sorry. And Chris' dad was curious about the new family who had
just moved in. Chris and Mae "made up" and went upstairs to play
while their dads talked in the living room. They invited each other
to their homes and a family-wide friendship started.

When Mae had problems, she ran to Chris' house. When Chris
started dating, Mae would "check out" the girls, asking around
who they were. One had a reputation, and Mae begged Chris not to
go out with her. It would ruin *his* reputation!

The two were inseparable, as close as brother and sister. They
played ice hockey together in the winter, roller bladed during the
summer, and were on the phone quite often, even though their

149

houses were only a few doors apart. Chris kept careful watch of Mae at their high school, teasing her about the boys who eyed her. She really was becoming a beautiful young lady. But more importantly, she was good at hockey. Chris and Mae played roller hockey during the summer so Chris could stay in shape. He lived and breathed hockey; he was going to play college hockey — it was his dream and he could feel it in his bones. He was one of the most valuable players on the team, and he felt he had a good chance to get to the university on a hockey scholarship.

It was Chris' sixteenth summer. Mae was all of fifteen, and they were planning to try out a new swimming spot at a lake with a group of their friends. She and Chris were excellent swimmers, and they were excited to go. The lake had a really cool hill that the kids slid down, and rocks jutted out at the top of the small hill. The gang thought it would be fun to jump off.

Sure enough, they were jumping and laughing in no time. Chris called out to Mae and prepared to do a swan dive, making exaggerated theatrical gestures. Mae yelled for him not to dive, but it was too late. Chris had jumped. The world was instantly silent. Time had stopped as Mae waited for Chris to come up. He didn't. It was about two minutes, and she thought maybe he was kidding, but he wasn't the type. He would sooner impress her than scare her. She screamed for everyone to look for Chris.

Chris broke his neck when he hit the lake bottom and lost consciousness under the water. His friends were able to pull him up and an air ambulance took him to a level-one trauma center thirty miles away. His chances were very slim for survival, the doctors said. Mae flew with him and was allowed to stay with him: she had told the doctors she was his sister and the gang had vouched for her. She made the necessary calls and returned to his side. Mae and Chris' parents never left his side those first few days. Chris was put on a respirator, underwent two surgeries, and spent two months in the hospital and seven months in rehab. Chris was in no pain, and he was able to move his head from side to side. Otherwise, he was paralyzed from the neck down.

Chris had to learn to eat again. It's quite a different story when you have to take what is offered to you. The spoon or fork may not be at the right angle or it may go in too deeply. Mae had to learn how to offer him his food, and Chris had to learn how to patiently give instructions that didn't offend people. A rhythm had to be established between breathing, eating, and drinking for Chris. The process took weeks to be successful.

At times during his hospital stay and during therapy in rehab, Chris had to fight depression, anger, sorrow, and denial. Each emotion came and went; it wasn't in a particular order. He was angry that he had jumped. He grieved over the loss of his future in hockey. He hoped maybe this was all a dream and at times believed he would walk again. But he knew better and at times depression would set in. A deep cloud would come over him, and he would have to take time to think and process what had happened to him. There were times when he saw no one and asked for understanding. He needed time to come to terms with God's role in this, with his future and all that had and wouldn't happen to him. It was quite a lot for a sixteen-year-old to handle.

There were times when Mae couldn't take it. She felt left out, shut out of Chris' world. But she knew she had to give him time, and she knew she couldn't step in for him. This was Chris' journey, this was Chris' battle, this was Chris' life. Pray as she might, she knew Chris could never, ever walk again. She would have to deal with it.

Looking back on these events, Chris tries to communicate to his audiences that although he would never wish this upon himself, he gained a deep understanding of life from this experience. He feels very blessed to be able to have had a profound feeling of the presence of God during this ordeal. He recalls sitting for hours in his wheelchair in the hospital, not wanting to see anyone, just thinking quietly, staring out the window at the world below. He knows God was with him. He could feel it. He could feel God's presence when he would cry uncontrollably, when he would struggle to breathe after the respirator was taken off, when he was trying to communicate what he needed to those who took care of him, and when he would see his dearest friend, Mae, crying for Chris.

Chris does not pity himself. He speaks all over the country, sharing how his faith was strengthened and warning children of

151

diving in untested areas. He speaks about the love of a dear friend, the dedication of his family, and the enormous strength he gained from his circle of friends from church and school.

While Mae would have wished that this could all be taken away from Chris, she also sees a different person in that wheelchair: a man who has grown to love God, a man who can still make a room full of people laugh at his jokes, and a man who has a passion for life.

Strike Three, You're Out!

" 'If another member of the church sins against you,
go and point out the fault when the two of you are alone.
If the member listens to you, you have regained that
one. But if you are not listened to, take one or two oth-
ers along with you, so that every word may be con-
firmed by the evidence of two or three witnesses. If the
member refuses to listen to them, tell it to the church.' "
(vv. 15-20)

It was a difficult issue: LaTonya was a beloved woman who
had been asked to watch the church nursery children ten years ago
when the church was desperate for help. She was paid well, both in
money and in food, and she kept coming back. She seemed to enjoy the job and continued to watch the children every week. LaTonya
thought it was a good situation.

But the new vicar had another view of the situation. Janna had
been there only two weeks when she eyed two little children running in and around the education wing on a Sunday morning. She
was about to preach her first sermon and had forgotten her notes in
her nervousness. In her hurry to get the notes, she took a shortcut
and ran through the deserted education wing. The children were in
church now, and the nursery was at the end of the wing. It was
quieter there, and there was a covered entrance where the children
could be dropped off and picked up. Janna wondered where LaTonya
and her young helpers were as she escorted the two two-year-olds
back to the nursery. LaTonya said she hadn't even noticed them
gone; she was watching television. This disturbed Janna.

But Janna was in a hurry and needed to get back to the sanctuary; she would talk to LaTonya later. LaTonya was already gone by
the time Janna had shaken hands, taken off her alb, and gathered

her materials. The church was empty, and Janna walked through the education wing with the senior pastor. She shared her concerns with Ron, and he suggested she call LaTonya at home that evening.

Janna thought it was a straightforward call, but the next morning two angry women were at the church door, insisting on knowing why Janna had questioned LaTonya's actions. A molehill had suddenly turned into a mountain. Some were calling it a racial issue. Others were calling it a personal attack. But Janna held strong and told them it was none of their business. She would take the matter up with LaTonya, Ron and, if necessary, the church council.

Janna was understandably upset at what was happening. She didn't want to alienate this woman, but the church was on a busy highway in a marginal area of town. Someone could have taken one of the children, and LaTonya wouldn't have known it. One of them could have run out on the highway, and LaTonya wouldn't have known it. It made Janna very upset that LaTonya refused to speak to her. She would only speak to Janna through a friend who was a lawyer. Janna thought it was terribly blown out of proportion.

LaTonya was not doing her job well at all. Several mothers came forward to say their children came home with diapers that were never changed. Some children had not been cleaned up after a snack and others came home with permanent marker stains on their clothing. In all, five mothers said they had left the church because the nursery was inadequate. Janna never knew and neither did the church council. Unfortunately, instead of complaining and bringing the complaints to light, the families simply left. The church council called each one to express their concern, apologize for what happened, and asked them to reconsider returning to the church. Other mothers shared that they took their children with them to church, although they would have preferred them to be in the nursery.

Indeed it was a big deal. Some sided with Janna and others sided with LaTonya. Ron suggested they fire LaTonya, but he had a feeling it wouldn't be that easy. LaTonya wanted a severance package before she left. Ron thought it was outrageous but knew the issue was getting out of hand and could pull some families away from the church.

Janna asked LaTonya to resign, but she refused. Janna approached the council and explained the situation in detail. LaTonya and her friends were also invited and gave their side of the story, saying Janna had been mistaken and the mothers who complained were exaggerating. In the end, the council felt the safety of the children was more important and fired LaTonya. They gave her one month's pay and asked her not to return the next Sunday. LaTonya was satisfied.

Two families left the church, but the council said if that's all it took for them to leave, then they weren't all that committed. They were concerned about LaTonya, but also relieved to know the children would be safe and watched over. And all this in Janna's first month of internship! It was quite an issue, but Janna handled it effectively, sharing it quietly, then with Ron and then with the council. She was left with no alternative. And the church was left with better supervision of the children.

Forgiveness

---

*"Then Peter came and said to him, 'Lord, if another
member of the church sins against me, how often should
I forgive? As many as seven times?' Jesus said to him,
'Not seven times, but, I tell you, seventy-seven times.' "
(vv. 21-22)*

Jessie worked at a grocery store after school. He skimped and
saved, working long hours to fulfill his dream of going to England.
He had been fascinated with England since his social studies class
in fourth grade, and it was his dream to go there after high school
graduation. Jessie wanted to see the world, starting with England.

Jessie made it to England and had a wonderful time hiking and
walking through the countryside. He met truly interesting and kind
people along the way and invited all of them to come to stay with
him when they came to America. He left them with promises to
write.

Jessie wrote and received letters from his new friends. One of
them asked him for money. The man needed money for surgery, it
was urgent, and he didn't know anyone else who could come up
with that kind of money. He promised Jessie he would be repaid
within the year. Jessie sent him three thousand dollars.

Jessie was successful in college, graduating in three and a half
years instead of four. All the long hours of studying and going to
summer school paid off: he was one of the youngest to pass the
bar. Jessie got on board with a successful law firm as a public de-
fense attorney. He didn't make as much as his colleagues, but he
knew it was a good solid beginning. He would eventually make
lots of money and travel. He had promised himself another major
trip after graduation. He wanted to go to Australia and New Zealand
to see kiwi and sheep farms, to see both clipper and cruise ships,

and to see both the waterfront and indigenous areas. He had studied the countries and couldn't wait to see them. But first he'd have to get a hold of those three thousand dollars he had loaned a few years ago after his trip to England. He never did hear from the fellow.

Jessie tried to contact him, but the man's phone number was out of order. He called information. No, there was no one living in the town with that name. He called the magistrate's office. No, there was a man with that name three or four years ago, but he was wanted on theft charges and had moved on. Jessie had been conned out of three thousand dollars.

Jessie had to make a decision. Should he pursue this matter further, at his own expense? Or should he just let it go? It irked him that he had been so dumb, but he had been on a high from traveling through England and Jessie in his excitement, loaned his transient friend the money.

Jessie would have to write it off as a learning experience. He'd have to forgive and forget about it.

Erring On The Side Of Compassion

---

*"'Friend, I am doing you no wrong; did you not agree
with me for the usual daily wage? Take what belongs to
you and go; I choose to give to these last the same as I
give to you. Am I not allowed to do what I choose with
what belongs to me? Or are you envious because I am
generous?' " (vv. 13-15)*

When I worked as an emergency assistance coordinator for
Lutheran Social Services, I made many errors — I hope on the side
of compassion. We had people who could tell me the most poi-
gnant stories, bringing me practically to tears, and then when I did
some research I found that all the details were lies. Some came to
me showing me scars and telling me story after story about abuse
or some violent act toward them. I could only remember that I was
there not to judge but to help.

Those who passed our first hurdle with my volunteers came to
talk to me in my office. About eighty percent were turned away at
the "gate" by my volunteers, many who know the regulars. But
those who came to see me were thought to have a legitimate need.
They had signed in, registered, given their identification (agency
policy, not mine), and had answered the preliminary questions. They
also had some proof of their problem.

No matter what they told me, I had decided that if they came to
me and would wait patiently to see me, then their problems must
be real. I realize it sounds a little naïve, but I had no way to check
out every story, and I needed a guide. My guide was that if they
were willing to wait, then they got assistance.

I was burned many, many times. One woman came for heating
assistance and showed me bills that were three months old, total-
ing almost 400 dollars. I felt sorry for her as she shivered in my

little office. I wrote out a check for 400 dollars. That afternoon at a community meeting, other social service agency managers and I were sharing stories and comparing notes. It seemed the lady had been to the Red Cross and Salvation Army and they each gave her 400 dollars. I was able to cancel my office's check by telephoning the bank before she cashed it. I saw her later that week driving a very stylish car. I felt taken advantage of, but I could have had no way of knowing.

Another man came to me for housing assistance, showing me past bills for medication for his wife, himself, and their handicapped older daughter. My heart went out to them because I recognized drugs for mental illness. They were very pricey. I committed to paying 1,000 dollars toward the rent. A few weeks later, he came in again with a completely different story, showed the same receipts, and was promptly refused by my volunteer, Roger, who recognized the guy. We were able to recoup the 1,000 dollars from his landlord because he had overpaid, and I felt fortunate to be able to use it for someone else.

But there were others who got help, and I will never know if they genuinely needed it or not. I have had women sit with me and cry as they told their sad tales. I have had men cry as they recounted terrible memories, strong pulls to a darker lifestyle or difficulties with addiction. I could not know if they were legitimate or not, and I made the decision, with the support of my board of directors, that I would rather err on the side of compassion than possibly turn a needy person away. I'm glad I did.

Some people complained, saying they needed more than the standard 25 dollars in grocery vouchers. They had more mouths to feed. I referred them to Social Services. Some complained they needed more than the fifteen dollars in gas vouchers I could provide. They had longer distances to go. I referred them to General Assistance.

It wasn't my place to play judge too much; I was there to give help. As an arm of the Lutheran church, I felt it more important to give people hope and a little help. Compassion cannot be replaced; cash can.

Petty Concerns

" 'Truly I tell you, the tax collectors and the prostitutes are going into the kingdom of God ahead of you. For John came to you in the way of righteousness and you did not believe him, but the tax collectors and the prostitutes believed him; and even after you saw it, you did not change your minds and believe him.' " (vv. 30-32)

Mitch loved his church. He loved tending the garden, cleaning up the yards, and planting flowers every spring. He made sure it looked spotless every Sunday morning.

One morning during adult Sunday school, Pastor Wangly asked the class if they were going to heaven. Some said they hoped so. Some said they weren't sure because they were still sinners. Some said they thought they would. Pastor Wangley asked Mitch. Mitch said that he felt he was a good Christian, that he was willing to spend hours and hours at church, and that he was surely going to heaven. Pastor Wangley challenged him.

"Mitch, do you think you are going to heaven because of all you do here at church?" Mitch nodded his head confidently. Yes, he did much around the church, paid for most of it out of his own pocket, and loved what he did for the church. The pastor praised Mitch for his efforts and reminded people that his work was beautiful — the lawns and flower beds were works of art. But Pastor Wangly also wanted to know about Mrs. So-and-so. Would she get to heaven if she never lifted a flower pot? Would she be able to go to heaven if she didn't "do" anything for the church? Time for the class was getting short, and Pastor Wangly surprised them by giving them homework. They were to concentrate on the question of who would get to heaven and why for the entire week and then come back next Sunday morning for discussion. Pastor Wangly got up to lead service; Mitch got up to make sure the sprinklers were reaching the west corner.

Mitch was bending over to pick up a dead flower when Mrs. Hanson walked up. "You do a beautiful job here, Mitch. I wish I had enough energy to tend the flowers like you do. We appreciate it. It's a joy to look at." Mitch smiled. Funny Mrs. Hanson. She was older than the hills — about 97 or 98 — and she was loved by everyone. She didn't remember much, but she knew everyone's names and what they did at church. Mitch wondered if she did anything at church.

It was communion Sunday that day and Mitch sat back in the fourth pew as he always did and watched as his fellow church members went up for communion. One by one they received Pastor Wangly's words: "The blood of Christ, shed for you; the body of Christ, given for you." It was like a mantra as Mitch heard the words over and over again. He began to reflect on the Sunday school assignment. Who would go to heaven?

Mitch saw the Warners get up to get communion. Karen polished the brass like no one else could in the altar guild. Surely she would go to heaven. But she had had a drug habit when she was young. Would she go to heaven?

Sandy got up with her three children. They were so cute. They were like stairsteps and the littlest one was about two years old. They loved coming to church — they sat on the first pew and quietly drew in their coloring books during the sermon. Surely they would go to heaven! But Sandy's children had different fathers. Would that count against her? Would she go to heaven?

Norm and Eugenia got up. They were a lovely couple. Always ready to offer their home to missionaries or visitors, they loved people and were very gracious. They were known for their hospitality. Yet in class today Norm was the one who said he "hoped" to go to heaven. Maybe he wouldn't?

As communion went on, Mitch asked himself if each person was going to heaven. Suddenly it hit him! It wasn't "what" the person did around church, in the community, or in the world. It

161

was "why" they did it. Mitch only had to turn to the person next to him to see a willing worker who was happy to help in any way. Wow! Some are busy doing busy work; others are genuinely interested in doing God's work.

A Steward Of Her Garden

" 'Therefore I tell you, the kingdom of God will be taken
away from you and given to a people that produces the
fruits of the kingdom.' " (v. 43)

Grace loves to garden and she tends her garden carefully. She
lives in a town of two million, in a quiet neighborhood in a three-
bedroom house with a nice backyard. She is happy where she is.

The environment is very important to Grace, who is a retired
geography teacher. Her husband is in the Alzheimer's unit at a
nearby hospital, and Grace uses her time to garden as her meditation time. She has lived a good life, and she is thankful for every
thing and every day she gets. She is grateful for her life of 81 years.

Grace is very careful about how she uses her garden space.
Tomatoes are planted and trained to grow upward in cages. Her
vines are tied to stakes with soft, discarded nylon stockings. Her
corn grows along the back wall, tall and proud. Grace spreads
torn newspaper under her cucumbers and pumpkins so they don't
get bruised or rotten. Her cantaloupe and watermelon lay on grass
clippings.

Grass clippings and other such things are collected in a wire
mesh "box" which Grace turns over with her shovel once a week.
It makes a nice mulch. Her compost pile is closer to the kitchen
and any vegetable peel, fruit seeds, or organic material is thrown
into it. She turns this pile over several times a week.

Fruits trees are numerous in her backyard. Grace makes sure
she doesn't use pesticides on her fruit trees. She doesn't want to
spoil the fruit, and she likes to hang birdhouses in the branches of
her trees. The birds feel secure there, knowing they can fly to the
cover of a branch if they need to. She fills her bird baths every

morning; the birds are certainly active in her neighborhood! They chirp happily as she comes out to garden each morning.

Grace also cares for the neighborhood squirrel family. She collects anything the squirrels can eat and puts it on tin pans at the edge of her garden. Sometimes when the grandkids come over, she fills pine cones with peanut butter and bird seed and she puts them along tree branches. Oh, do the squirrels ever make a racket when they see those pine cones!

Happiness and simplicity are words for Grace while she is in her garden. And maybe tranquil and contemplative would describe her also. Her world outside these garden walls is filled with the grief of her husband's disease and ill health. But inside, she thanks God for another day, recounts all her many, many blessings, and takes care of her little corner of the world.

Is It Too Late?

" 'For many are called, but few are chosen.' " (v. 14)

Courtney worried for her daughter. Lindsey was ten years old, and she was constantly looking in the mirror and telling herself that she didn't want to get fat. Courtney knew that looking in the mirror at this age is normal, for the onset of puberty is eagerly awaited at this stage. But the incessant comments about weight lay heavily on Courtney. Courtney knew why. She herself was heavy: she tipped the scales at 353 pounds. It was so embarrassing to go to the doctor because they had to bring in a special scale. Last time she was escorted to the sports acceleration weight room to be weighed — in front of all those kids who were training and exercising! Courtney went home that day and ate a whole bag of donuts. All 24 of them.

It didn't help though. Courtney knew she had a serious problem, but her doctor was a young man who said she should just "not eat as much." He said she should watch what she eats, write it down, and then realize how much she is eating. Like that's going to ever happen. But the HMO she belonged to didn't allow her to go to a specialist unless her primary care physician referred her, and he told her to tighten her belt, so to speak. But Courtney was continually loosening her belt as she gained more and more weight. Her stomach was flabby and it lopped over her pants. Her pants were stretch fabric: nothing else could stay up. She hated it. She hated being fat, and she hated herself for it.

But she loved Lindsey. Lindsey was her only child, and she would do anything for her. That's why, when Courtney caught Lindsey's continuous glances at her profile, Courtney sought help. Professional help from someone who would understand. Not some skinny little doctor who hadn't a clue about obesity.

Courtney went to a weight specialist and paid for it herself. At first she was required only to write everything down that she ate, the time, and what her mood was. She didn't have to eat less; in fact, the doctor told her it would benefit Courtney if she tried to eat as normally as she could.

And so she did. Then the hard part came next. Courtney was given vitamins and minerals to help curb her appetite. But they were not going to make her thinner. That was up to Courtney. Courtney had to learn why she ate what and when.

With a supervised diet, exercise, and weekly counseling sessions, Courtney began to lose weight. She spoke honestly with the doctor and was able to confront some unresolved issues left over from her childhood, which was for the most part happy. Courtney realized that she didn't eat to satisfy a physical hunger; Courtney ate to feed an emptiness inside her, an emotional hunger.

Lindsey also came to visit at the clinic and learned about proper food choices. She learned that she didn't have to become obese like her mother, which was Lindsey's greatest fear. And Lindsey learned how to eat to live, not to live to eat.

The two are making great progress. Lindsey is becoming a beautiful young woman who is proud of her body and who takes good care of herself. She doesn't feel that she needs to be a certain size or wear certain clothes to fit in. She is learning to trust herself to be the special person she is.

And Courtney is also making progress. She has lost 162 pounds so far. Her goal weight for her 5'2" frame is 145 pounds. She has only 46 pounds to go and knows she will make it. It's been two years now, and the difference has been incredible. Courtney feels better, not to mention looks much better, and is gaining confidence in herself. She hadn't realized that she was becoming somewhat of a hermit because of the embarrassment over her looks. Now she is learning to take care of the body that God gave her, the body that God loves, the body that she is learning to love.

The Debate Over Paying Social Security

" 'Give therefore to the emperor the things that are the emperor's, and to God the things that are God's.' "
(v. 21)

A group of farmers refused to pay taxes. They claim that when they are older, there will be no Social Security benefits, so why should they pay into it? They haven't paid Social Security in years, and they don't intend to start now.

Their pastor challenged them. He was new. He was young, fresh out of seminary. He didn't know anything.

The men laughed at his question. "Why shouldn't you pay into Social Security?" he had asked them innocently, taking another bite of his caramel roll. The men were sitting in the town café. It was coffee time, and Pastor Ed never missed his caramel roll and hot chocolate. It was like a sacred ritual. It was his comfort food, he said. No one could make caramel rolls better than his late mother, and these were pretty close.

Pastor Ed repeated his question. "Why shouldn't you pay into Social Security?" The men squirmed in the chairs at the long table that ran down the center of the café. Hadn't he been listening? Didn't he understand that when he was old and gray he wouldn't get the benefit of Social Security? How could they explain this to him?

Waldo, who was eating an omelette, was the first to try. He paused and waved his fork in the air. "Pastor Ed, there won't be any money in there when I'm old, much less for when you are old. Why would we pay into it if we don't get anything out of it?" Ed kept eating his roll, thoroughly enjoying it. He was listening.

George piped in. "Yeah, and the way the government is squandering it now anyway, people won't even remember what Social

Security was by the time we're 65." He looked at Ed. Ed licked his thumb.

Roland was sure he could make the new pastor understand. "Pastor Ed, it's like this. If we pay into it, we won't get anything in return. We'll be throwing our money away. Why, we could just as well be throwing our money to the wind!" Roland took a loud slurp of his coffee and yelled for more.

"Hm. But what if someone needs the money?" Pastor Ed looked at the men. He wanted to know where they were coming from.

"Well," said Hugh, "they can get a job! Even at McDonald's if they have to!" He smiled at the thought. "Sometimes I'd like to work at McDonald's on those days when it's forty below with the wind howling in my ears and I'm trying to feed the cows. Man, it's wicked around here in January and February!"

Ed smiled. "I know. Did you know that I grew up in South Dakota? That's not too far away. I moved here from Louisiana, but I grew up in South Dakota. I know what winters are like. They can be rough."

The men were amazed. They didn't know Ed was from South Dakota! They were all excited and had many questions for Ed, all at once. Why did he leave South Dakota? And what was in Louisiana? Did he like it here in Minnesota?

Ed put his hand up. "Let me just tell you that I was born and reared in the Black Hills where the wind can come off the hills and tear right through to your soul. My mom and dad died in a car accident when I was fourteen, and I went to live with my aunt. But she was in a wheelchair, and her husband didn't care too much about me — or her for that matter. I was a ward of the state until I was seventeen, when I went to college on a basketball scholarship. I graduated from Louisiana State and then headed for seminary. I always knew I wanted to be a pastor, and I went right for it. I'm one who is glad for Social Security. Without Social Security, I would have been homeless. I was able to live off my Social Security check right until I finished college. It paid for my food and books."

The men were silent. Ed was called to the phone. Mr. Olson was going into the hospital again. He had to go. Ed tossed down a twenty-dollar bill on the table. "It's my pleasure, gentlemen; coffee is on me today."

He headed out the door. He was hoping the men would think about his words.

Being Neighborly

"He said to him, 'You shall love the Lord your God
with all your heart, and with all your soul, and with all
your mind.' This is the greatest and first commandment.
And a second is like it: 'You shall love your neighbor
as yourself.' On these two commandments hang all the
law and the prophets." (vv. 37-40)

Bea is 81, but you would never know it looking at her. Bea
walks the mall every day, making sure she gets in her two miles.
She doesn't walk particularly fast, but she walks steadily. Bea has
energy and takes good care of herself, and walking makes her feel
good. Besides, in the harsh northern plains, walking season lasts
only six months!

Bea has never worked outside the home; her husband was a
doctor and they could afford for her to stay home to bring up their
daughter and son. She loves to bring treats to her neighbors and
has coffee daily with a widow woman across the street. She doesn't
live a fancy lifestyle, but she is generous in her giving. Neighbor
children know she will never turn them away when they come to
sell things for school or scouts.

Last winter, two days before Christmas, Bea was walking home
from her neighbor's house — after coffee — when she slipped on
a patch of ice. She broke her shoulder. It was very painful and her
recovery was long.

Bea was in the hospital two weeks, and a physical therapist
came for a few weeks after to make sure Bea knew how to reach
for things and didn't injure herself. Bea hated being so inactive.
She had planned to have the children over for Christmas. Instead,
they came to the hospital and celebrated in her room. It wasn't the
same, but Bea has to admit it was unique, with visitors streaming

in and out for days. It was fun to have so much commotion, and she jokingly says she was glad not to have to clean up before and after the guests arrived!

When Bea returned from the hospital, her walkway was scraped clean. Her driveway was cleaned and shoveled, and the path from the garage to the kitchen door was cleared. A thick, industrial outdoor mat was carefully laid between the door and the garage. There was no chance Bea would slip on its secure base.

During the winter months, Bea saw neighbors come to shovel, scrape, and blow the snow away. Even though she wasn't going anywhere for a while, her driveway was always carefully cleared. Bea still cries when she shares that she would be sitting at her kitchen table eating and she would see neighbors tending to her yard or bringing her food. She called them often to tell them how much she appreciated it. Every time they declared they were "just being neighborly."

That spring was unusually wet. Bea stepped out one morning to find a newspaper tube hung next to her door. All she had to do was open the door and right at the same level as the door handle hung a newspaper tube. A piece of roof gutter was attached and the water was drained to the back, into the bushes. What a clever idea!

Her neighbors take good care of her, and when she asks them if she can pay them, they laugh. They recall all the times she has brought them meals, all the times she would joyfully babysit their children, all the times she and her husband gave them candy as they took their evening walk.

What a testimony! What a joy! What wonderful neighbors to have!

Should He Or Shouldn't He?

" 'The greatest among you will be your servant. All
who exalt themselves will be humbled, and all who
humble themselves will be exalted.' " (vv. 11-12)

Gilbert was about to graduate from seminary. He got his regional assignment and his first call request and was making preparations to visit the church. He had to pack, take his finals, and get all his paperwork in order so he and his wife could make the move from Texas to Arizona. Gilbert, a former science teacher, was 48 and had put his schooling on hold until his children were grown and gone. He was eager to go: he had wanted to teach and preach for a long time, and he was glad he was finished with the schooling part of his career. He couldn't wait to get settled in and serve as pastor.

Gilbert met the senior pastor and two associate pastors. Gilbert considered their offer. Gilbert would be in charge of adult education and visitation if he took the call. It sounded just like what he loved to do. He bought many cleric shirts, both long- and short-sleeved. He bought a new alb with matching band, and his cinctures hung ready. He wanted to make sure to look the part. He loved the fancy appointments that came with the job of pastor!

Gilbert was very surprised that first Sunday when he and his wife came to visit. He was just expected to sit and observe the service. He would be introduced, and there was a potluck in his honor after the service. The church wanted him to feel at ease. Pastor Tim, the senior pastor, and Karen, the first associate pastor, got up to do the service. Pastor Tim was wearing a black cleric and dark gray trousers. Karen was wearing a dress. No alb. No suit coat. No fancy vestments. Gilbert was confused, but he didn't say anything. The service included lots of singing and praying, and it was made easier with a large screen up at the front of the church. There was no need for bulletins. Gilbert missed the baptismal font.

The service was very, very casual, and Gilbert was disappointed and felt like he missed true worship. He wanted to hear liturgy. He wanted to hear more of what he was used to. He would have to be flexible, he told himself, if he expected himself to fit in.

Pastor Tim and Gilbert visited long into the afternoon after the scrumptious potluck. Pastor Tim wanted Gilbert to feel comfortable and tried to let him in on things. Pastor Karen, too, came and sat with them and helped shed light on many of their traditions at St. Stephen. She brought up the absence of vestments.

The congregation was older but was trying to attract younger people. Being in the heart of "sun country" and having such an elderly population brought the average church member's age up to 63. Many came from northern states and were there only for the winter. St. Stephen Church wanted to attract younger people so the church wouldn't be so deserted in the winter.

Gilbert took the call. He hardly ever wears his alb during regular worship services, but he does at every funeral, wedding, and baptism. He wants to make sure to distinguish that for him being dressed the part gives him confidence to proclaim the good news. Even though he realizes that one can wear jeans and a t-shirt and still proclaim the gospel, Gilbert is a little old-fashioned. He likes to look the part, dress the part, and act the part.

His alb still hangs in the vestry, ready in case it is needed.

The Wise And The Foolish Bridesmaids

" 'Keep awake therefore, for you know neither the day nor the hour.' " (v. 13)

Jacopo Tintoretto paints a stunning portrayal of The Parable of The Wise and The Foolish Virgins. Painted in oil around the year 1548, the painting gives much attention to the stance of the bridesmaids, both the foolish group and the wise group. Tintoretto's interpretation of the parable is beautiful.

The painting is mainly an olive green, depicting a huge courtyard with a long, wide balcony above spanning the length of the courtyard. On the second floor one sees the ballroom with a beautiful chandelier hanging in the center. The ceiling of the ballroom is painted, resembling an oriental rug. The windows on the second floor are arched at the top and reach toward the ceiling. A room is seen off to the side where food is being placed on a table covered with cloth. Men and women alike are both standing idle and dancing in the ballroom.

The upper balcony is edged in wrought iron, upon which lean the wise bridesmaids, the bride and the bridegroom. The group is looking down at the women in the courtyard. They wear fine dresses of velvet. Lace adorns their necklines, and they wear Chantilly lace veils upon their heads. They lean over the wrought iron railing, as if in conversation with the group below. Their mouths are open.

The courtyard below seems vast with beautiful tile on the ground. There are designs in the tile and the side of the courtyard leads to hallways. The halls are clearly visible. A couple is walking in one of the halls, apparently to a room on the side of the mansion. They are dressed in fine clothing.

A man leans his hand high on the wall in the other hallway. He is dressed in dark clothing, but has a shawl or cloak draped at his hips. He looks as if he needs assistance to stand. He is looking toward the group of bridesmaids in the center of the courtyard.

Five bridesmaids stand in various poses in the middle of the courtyard. They all look up toward the group leaning over the balcony railing. Their faces are twisted in pain or anguish as they consider the events upstairs.

One leans over a bowl where a small dog sits. It looks as if she is going to pour oil in the bowl. The little dog looks on, interested.

Another woman holds a lamp and is poised to walk on. But she hesitates and stands with one knee up, as if frozen. Her body is fully visible against the clingy fabric of her dress. But it does not matter. She is not going upstairs.

One can imagine what another woman is doing. She holds a lantern in one hand and has her other hand outstretched toward the group on the balcony. She is begging to go up. She, too, is dressed in a beautiful gown with lace at her neck and on her head. But her hand is reaching to no avail. She will not be allowed in.

A bridesmaid is tortured, standing with hips thrust forward, arms held back and face looking upward. Her expression is one of agony as she considers that she will not be let in.

Holding the train of her long veil, another bridesmaid seems resigned to the fact that she cannot get upstairs. She is looking upward, but her body stands as if she is turning back, away from the entrance to the ballroom upstairs. She knows she is not allowed in.

A room is at the back of the entrance to the upstairs. It's hard to see what is in the room other than a man and woman sitting on the floor, kneeling. They seem to look over the courtyard in annoyance at the noise the bridesmaids must be making.

As with Jesus in telling this parable, the message Tintoretto paints is obvious: the foolish will fail; the wise will triumph.

Burying Or Multiplying Riches

---

*" 'For it is as if a man, going on a journey, summoned
his slaves and entrusted his property to them; to one
he gave five talents, to another two, to another one, to
each according to his ability. Then he went away.' "
(vv. 14-15)*

In Jesus' day, it was rabbinical law that if you had a sure treasure, you could bury it for safekeeping. If it was stolen, you would be excused of any liability the treasure may cause. But if you hid it, it was assumed that your treasure would not increase. If you took a risk and made it multiply, then you were the wiser one. Your talents could grow and your profit would increase.

In this parable, Jesus was assuring the people that God would prefer a return on his investment and would welcome risk takers!

Our church had a clever, if not original, idea for stewardship. The Stewardship Committee handed out envelopes with ten-dollar bills enclosed. They were to be used at a person's discretion and returned in about three months as an exercise of applying their talents. A dynamic sermon was given on the topic of being "God's money managers." It was exciting to hear that as God had invested in our lives, so we could invest our money for the good of the church.

The opportunity to participate was purely voluntary, but not many of the 350 envelopes were turned down. The church was investing 3,500 dollars. The members could return as much or as little of this investment as they wanted.

Periodic updates were given during the following three months to see how people were using "God's money" and what their returns were looking like. Enthusiasm was mounting as the time for the "Talent Return" was nearing. A special service was held in which people got up and shared exactly what they did and how they made their money grow (or how it failed to grow in a few cases). A total of 18,491 dollars was returned to the church.

A contest was held at the end of the service to see who was the most creative, the most frugal, the most rewarding monetarily, the one who tried the hardest, and a few other categories. The awards ceremony was about as much fun as the entire project!

Following are some of the winning ideas that members used to make their money grow:

1. The money was used to buy craft supplies and crafts were made and sold for a 320-dollar profit.

2. A beautiful harbor-front home was turned into a Bed & Breakfast for two weekends with the ten dollars used for breakfast ingredients for a 480-dollar profit (this couple won the "Most Rewarding" award).

3. The money was used to buy ingredients for a fancy meal and two tickets were sold at fifty dollars each for the chance to eat this meal. The member is a chef at an elegant restaurant. The profit was ninety dollars.

4. Ingredients were bought to make lefse, a potato-based flat dough that resembles a tortilla. Forty dozen lefse rounds were sold at two dollars per dozen for a seventy-dollar profit.

5. One young man bought a very broad, strong rake and raked leaves for a 315-dollar profit (he won the "Most Innovative" award!).

6. One woman snipped her houseplants and bought small pots (ten for one dollar) with her ten dollars. She sold 100 small plants at three dollars and fifty cents each for a profit of 340 dollars.

7. One teenager and her mother bought window-cleaning supplies and washed windows at five dollars per window for a profit of 310 dollars.

8. One young man bought nothing with his ten dollars but offered to walk dogs along the beach. He made a 300-dollar profit.

9. One woman, who loves to organize parties, organized a potluck. She bought paper goods and decorations and hand-wrote name cards. Forty-three people came to her potluck for an entry fee of five dollars each person. She made 205 dollars in profit.

10. One couple spent ten dollars on fancy signs and had a neighborhood garage sale. They brought in almost 5,000 dollars for the church and won the "Most Successful" award.

11. One family gave a concert. The father and son play guitar, the mother plays piano, one daughter plays flute, and the other daughter plays violin. They used their ten dollars for refreshments and charged three dollars per person. They raised 401-dollars profit.

12. One elderly lady crocheted an afghan, using her money for yarn. She sold raffle tickets for five dollars at a summer concert and netted 375 dollars.

13. One lady offered to babysit for three weekends. Her return was 85 dollars.

14. One group of teenage girls went around to church members' homes for four weeks and offered to put garbage cans back in their holders for one dollar per can. They raised 198 dollars.

15. The pastor didn't use his ten dollars. Instead, he offered not to give a sermon for the highest bid. His profit was 1,350 dollars!

Reformed Thinking

"We are descendants of Abraham and have never been slaves to anyone. What do you mean by saying, 'You will be made free'?" (v. 33)

Tom doesn't like black people. It is the belief of many of his friends that Tom dislikes this group because he doesn't know anyone who is black. It's such an archaic notion to dislike a particular group because of color, background, gender, or religion, but Tom says he can't help himself.

Otherwise, Tom is a pretty nice guy. He works hard, helps around church and his community, adores his wife and children, and is very outgoing. He just doesn't like black people. His friends have challenged him time and again to no avail. Tom couldn't change his way of thinking.

Until Tom met Rebekkah.

Tom's oldest daughter, Tina, wanted to adopt a baby. She and her husband had tried to conceive for six years. Tina worked in a hospital; her husband, Rollie, worked for a trucking company as an auditor. They had a very comfortable life, but they felt they were missing something. They wanted a baby in their lives. They wanted someone to love, nurture, and share their happy marriage with. They signed up for a home study.

A few changes had to be made to pass the home study, but a new fence, different locks, and gadgets here and there were nothing compared to the excitement they had over the prospect of having a little one around their home. Rollie would have bought a whole new house had the state wanted it!

The adoption agency called one evening. Would they consider taking in a foster child? The agency said they were desperate for this child to have a home for at least a month or two until they could find an adoptive home for her; the child was a newborn. Would Tina and Rollie consider it? Tina and Rollie didn't hesitate, although they reminded the agency to continue searching for a baby for them. The state worker would bring the baby over within the hour, and they could sign temporary custody papers later. Tina and Rollie were happy, even though they knew it was to be a temporary situation.

Rebekkah was all bundled up in her infant seat when she came. The worker, Mrs. Williams, took her out and handed her over to Tina and gave Rollie papers to sign.

Tina held Rebekkah in her arms. Rebekkah was four days old and had been abandoned at the county hospital. The state would look for her mother, but the chances were very good Rebekkah would be in foster care until she could be adopted. The hospital had discovered that the name the mother had used was false, her address was the address of a museum, and Mrs. Williams didn't hold out hope for finding the mother. "And if we do, I can't imagine she would want this child. The mother was only fourteen years old and took great pains to leave the hospital in secret. At least she named the baby! Oh, I just changed Rebekkah, so she should be all right for a good while." Mrs. Williams said she would come back in a few days with the custody papers.

Tina held Rebekkah tighter, rocking her through the night. She didn't want to let her go, and she sat in the living room with only the night light on for several hours. The next morning, Tina unwrapped Rebekkah and changed her. She had taken two little bottles of milk through the night and Tina wanted to see her little friend closer. Rebekkah's skin was dark, her eyelashes were long, the bridge of her nose was a little flat, and her mouth puckered up as if sucking. Tina knew she was the most beautiful baby in the world. How would she be able to give her up after only a few months?

Tina and Rollie took turns holding Rebekkah, singing to her, and watching her sleep in her little bassinet by the couch. They just couldn't seem to keep their eyes off her, and they wanted to hold her every minute. What on earth would they do when they adopted their own child? They laughed together at the thought.

The state couldn't find Rebekkah's mother and Tina and Rollie filed for permanent custody after only two weeks. They just couldn't bear the thought of their little Rebekkah living with any other family. They loved her too much.

Tina's family came to look at the baby and brought her a mountain of presents. Tiny pink dresses with ruffles and bows, a rocking horse that would have to wait for many months, a pair of little red leather shoes, and many, many more things were showered upon Rebekkah. Their families were so happy for them!

Except for Tom. He took one look at Rebekkah and gasped. He wouldn't even hold her. "She's black — well, part black anyway! Give her back!" Tina was appalled at her father's comment. "Her mother is white. And who cares anyway? You don't know if she's black. Her skin is dark, but her father could have been Latino! Or Filipino! Or — who cares!" Tina was incensed. She ran to her room and cried. Tom ran up after her. He apologized, but told her he just didn't like black people. Tina told him to get out and never come back unless he could accept Tina, Rollie, and Rebekkah as a family.

Tom was hurt, deeply hurt. He loved his oldest daughter, but why did they have to do this to him? He talked to his pastor and his friends. They were very concerned and warned him not to come between his daughter and granddaughter. "Don't make her choose because you'll lose," they warned. Tom had to think long and hard about it.

He avoided the house when Tina came over with Rebekkah — which was often. Tina's mother and two sisters couldn't stop talking about little Rebekkah, and Tom had to admit he was curious.

Rebekkah was at his house when Tom came in one day after work. He had forgotten that Rollie and Tina had to go to a banquet and Tom's wife was going to watch Rebekkah. Tom could hear his wife in the kitchen, humming and banging pots. Tom peeked under the hood of the bassinet. Rebekkah's hand was by her mouth and her mouth was making a little sucking noise. Was she hungry? What if she was? But she wasn't crying, she must be dreaming, he thought. He lifted the blanket a little. Her little legs were round and chubby. He squeezed her little thigh — oh, he remembered when the girls were this age! He loved to sit and hold them for hours. He had held them and played with them and read to them until his wife teased him that he forgot she existed. Tom remembered how fun it was to have a baby around. They were so precious!

Tom looked at Rebekkah long and hard. Why was his heart so hardened? This was a baby who needed a family. Why was he so mean and biased? He reached down and picked up little Rebekkah. She was sleeping soundly and he cradled her in his arm and sat on the recliner. Carefully, he wrapped a blanket around her and he put his feet up. It had been a long day, he was tired, but he wanted to hold Rebekkah for a little while.

Tina eyed her dad on the recliner, holding Rebekkah, when she and Rollie came to get her a few hours later. Tom was snoring softly, and she hated to wake him up, but Tina wanted to get home. She winked at her mother, who was reading a book on the couch nearby. "I tell you, I don't understand your father," her mother said. "All this talk about not wanting to have anything to do with Rebekkah and I come in here and who's on the recliner sleeping, holding Rebekkah? You'd think he was getting soft in his old age."

Tom woke up and kissed Rebekkah. Tina could see he had been crying. He admitted he was praying and thinking, and with every breath Rebekkah took, he felt himself falling deeper and deeper in love with her. His little granddaughter had won his heart when she looked up and smiled up at him.

"Dad, that must have been an air bubble. She doesn't smile yet!" But Tina smiled and thanked her dad for holding Rebekkah. "She's a beauty, isn't she? She's so sweet and only needs one bottle through the night. We're all getting more sleep. I think I'm getting this mother business down, Dad."

He looked at his daughter and reached out to her. "Well, maybe I'm getting this grandfather business down, too!"

All Saints' Sunday
Matthew 5:1-12

The Fullness Of Life

"Rejoice and be glad, for your reward is great in heaven,
for in the same way they persecuted the prophets who
were before you." (v. 12)

Some in our generation grew up hearing about World War II. We can't relate too much because we weren't there, but we have heard stories and understand the horrific events that took place. Some people came out okay; others did not make it out alive. But everyone who has been through it has been changed forever. Some are stronger; some can never recover; some are outspoken; some are prisoners in their own silence.

One story has touched the hearts of many as a woman shared her story from riches to rags to riches again. She feels she has been blessed to be through the war because she knows the tragedy it brings, the preciousness of life, and the opportunity it gave her to make every second count. She has a fullness of life about her.

Willy, as her friends call her, was born in southern Germany and was a teenager during the war. Her father was a clock maker, renowned for his intricate work and the ability to fix just about any timepiece that came his way. Her mother died when she was young, and Willy was very close to her father. The only problem was that her father was Jewish. They lived in a beautiful flat with mahogany furniture made especially for the rooms. The parlor was draped in pink and maroon velvets. Gold brocade and fringe accented much around the home. Her mother had an eye for decorating, and her father's wealth allowed the home to be beautifully appointed.

Willy was driven to private school across town by the family driver. She wore fur coats to ward off the chilly German air, and her shoes were polished daily. Willy admits she lived a life of luxury when she was young.

But the war changed that. Her father was killed in a concentration camp, and Willy escaped to Holland, where she was passed off as a daughter of a Dutch family. She was not bothered. She went to school with the children of the family, riding their bicycles along the canals in Voorburg. She wore dresses that were handed down through the family and thought they looked wonderful! Willy grew up remembering what it was like to have only a piece of cheese and a half a slice of bread for supper. She was poor living with this family; but she was rich. She had her life. She had her faith. She was going to live her life to the fullest!

Willy grew up to marry a wealthy entrepreneur who owned a chain of hotels. They eventually moved to the east coast and the business took care of itself. But Willy never forgot the kindness of her Dutch family, sending for them often to come and see the sights. She also visited them many times over the years until the children — her "siblings" — all grew up.

At the age of sixty, Willy wanted to leave behind a legacy, not for her own glory, but to honor her father and her adoptive family. She started a scholarship fund for students of German, Jewish, or Dutch ancestry. They would have the opportunity to be awarded thousands of dollars toward their education. The only catch was they had to get high marks and write an essay on what it meant to live life to its fullest. Willy got funny letters from people saying living life to its fullest meant spending lavishly, getting the most out of life they could. That wasn't even close to what she had in mind.

Willy received many truly thoughtful letters from young people who felt living life to its fullest included reaching out to others, helping where they could in their own communities, or changing negative thoughts. Willy has single-handedly sponsored many scholarships — full scholarships — to several young men and women. She loves to tell their stories.

One is a young woman who was born with a cleft palate. Her family was poor, and a team of doctors operated on her free of charge. Ruby was an excellent student and used Willy's scholarship to go an Ivy League school. She is now a doctor who works in

Brazil, where babies born with cleft palates are a particularly common problem. Her clinic is sponsored by churches, and she and her team are able to help many children each month. She feels she is living life to its fullest.

Willy gets a kick out of Jeremy, who learned what it is like to be a prisoner at the ripe age of ten. He wrote Willy a letter saying that the fullness of life meant staying out of juvenile hall. He was in and out of foster care until he spent seven years straight in a juvenile facility. His loneliness made him swear that he would grow up to make a difference for children. He is now a successful lawyer in a large town. He works in family law.

Willy has many, many more stories like these besides her own. Willy could have been killed in Germany — or even in Holland had her identity been revealed. She regrets her father's death, but she also wants to go on with life. She chooses to give so that others may give and be of service in their professions. She hopes gifts of scholarships will make a difference.

Thanksgiving Day
Luke 17:11-19

Leprosy

---

*"As Jesus entered a village, ten lepers approached him.
Keeping their distance, they called out, saying, 'Jesus,
Master, have mercy on us!' When he saw them, he said
to them, 'Go and show yourselves to the priests.' And
as they went, they were made clean." (vv. 12-14)*

Leprosy is a horrendous skin condition, a mycobacterial disease. It is caused by a parasite, and in the twenty-first century, more than twelve million people carry the parasite. Leprosy today is known as Hansen's disease, after the man who discovered the parasite. The parasite is transmitted by intimate contact, usually with a household member. The incubation period can be from one to two years to forty years. Its origin is very difficult, if not impossible at times, to determine.

Complications from leprosy are usually due to peripheral nerve involvement resulting from either infection or neuritis. A person with leprosy does not register pain and secondary infections are also common. Eye problems can lead to glaucoma and blindness. Today, treatments such as chemotherapy, physiotherapy, and reconstructive surgery may correct many of the disabilities.

In Jesus' day, chemotherapy, physiotherapy, and reconstructive surgery were not used to treat leprosy. The lepers were simply shunned — banned from society. If a person with leprosy was well enough to go out, he or she had to yell, "Unclean!" so that people could distance themselves from the leper. Their clothes had to be torn so that they could be readily identified. They were outcasts in every sense of the word.

In Jesus' time a cure included boiling or burning clothes. The book of Leviticus gives clear instructions of the cleansing of a leper and certifying his or her recovery of health. Bathing, shaving, and animal sacrifice were part of the "cure." Oil had to be administered once healed, as well as a burnt sin offering brought to the temple. But the most important ingredient was the declaration from a priest.

Leprosy was a dreaded plague then, bringing horror and despair to the sufferer, with little hope for reentry into society. But we read in this passage that Jesus, when approached by a group of lepers, spoke to them. Jesus was greeted with the word "Master." And instead of crying out, "Unclean!" the lepers cry out for mercy. Jesus does not touch them, and he does not give them instructions other than to tell them to go before the priests. In this passage, the lepers go and on their way they realize they are healed — completely healed of this horrendous condition. They are elated! It is truly a miracle.

Did the nine who didn't thank Jesus think that he had nothing to do with their cure? The priests were the only ones who were able to declare the lepers clean. The priests had to examine them and give them permission to be regular members of the society at large. Priests were the only ones who could establish the lepers as well and allow them back into the religious community and community at large.

I bet they didn't even think that Jesus had anything to do with it.

Only one of the ten turns back to Jesus. The man is a Samaritan, someone who is not supposed to be speaking to a Jew. But he turns to Jesus and calls out in a loud voice, praising God. He falls down before Jesus and thanks him. Only the stranger, the foreigner, gives thanks to Jesus for curing him. He recognizes Jesus' power; the man had received not only healing but divine grace.

If we have no faith, then God can't work in our lives. The Samaritan had faith. He allowed God to work in his life. He was cured. And he was thankful.

Christ The King
Matthew 25:31-46

Fred's Team

"Then the king will say to those at his right hand,
'Come, you who are blessed by my Father, inherit the
kingdom prepared for you from the foundation of the
world; for I was hungry and you gave me food, I was
thirsty and you gave me something to drink, I was a
stranger and you welcomed me, I was naked and you
gave me clothing, I was sick and you took care of me, I
was in prison and you visited me.' " (vv. 34-36)

Every day newspapers, magazines, and radio stations report how "bad" things are getting. There is a negative atmosphere around the general daily news. People are killing each other for no reason. Retaliations are more fierce than ever. Drug use, teen pregnancy, and television violence emphasize that the moral meter is headed in a downward spiral. We are going downhill is the consensus of many.

But we don't have to look very far to see the other side of the equation. Ordinary people do extraordinary things. There are countless unsung heroes who do things that will help others, both directly and indirectly. There are also public heroes whose legacies continue to help others. One example is Fred Lebow, founder of the New York Marathon.

Who would run a five-borough marathon to commemorate a sixtieth birthday? Fred Lebow would. He did — and his sixtieth birthday happened to fall two years after his diagnosis of brain cancer. All told, he ran 69 marathons in over thirty countries in his running career.

Mr. Lebow started running to build up endurance for tennis, which was his diversion after long hours working in the garment industry. Mr. Lebow started the New York Runners Club in 1970 with 126 runners. Ten years later, in 1980, over 16,000 runners entered the New York Marathon. Later the club reached more than 31,000 runners under Mr. Lebow's direction. He was president of the New York Runners twenty years before being promoted to chairman.

Mr. Lebow was born in Transylvania, Romania, in 1932. He lived in both Ireland and Czechoslovakia before coming to the United States. He lived in New York and worked as a textile consultant in the garment district. He left his consulting career when he became more involved in the business side of the Marathon.

Running is seen by some as boring, unprofitable, and too solitary and routine. Yet, there are many who love the competition and the endurance running gives and the spiritual component of training those long hours. Many argue that it's the perfect sport: the only required investment is a good pair of running shoes, it's possible to do just about anywhere, and it can be done with or without others. Marathon races themselves have a festive air to them with team T-shirts, medals, refreshments, and lots of publicity. Fans and runners get excited at a marathon, and there is much opportunity for pride in beating a personal best time.

Running used to be a blue collar sport, but under Mr. Lebow's direction, running in New York became fashionable. Upper-class runners touted their personal well-being. Middle-class runners liked the social status. No matter the socioeconomic status, running for countless people gives a much better health outlook. People claim to have regularity, better sex lives, and a rosier outlook on life when they run. Many who travel constantly combat jet lag with jogging. It seems it gets under one's skin, and the pull to run is overwhelming.

Mr. Lebow recognized the benefits of running and, with corporate sponsorships and larger numbers of runners, saw the New York Marathon blossom into a well-respected race. Its organizers were former volunteers; now they are paid executives. The New York Marathon is a business venture with a salaried staff.

Mr. Lebow recognized that women wanted a shorter, more manageable run. He suggested a road race in sections which quickly grew to become the famous Mini-Marathon. The "Mini," as it fondly became known, is a 6.2-mile, or 10-kilometer run and drew over 6,000 runners in the first few years. It has grown and become a favorite for many women.

Fred Lebow did much for the sport of marathoning. He was inducted into the United States Track & Field Hall of Fame a few months before he died in 1994 of brain cancer. He also raised millions of dollars for cancer research before his death.

Mr. Lebow received care at the Sloan-Kettering Cancer Center in New York and both the Cancer Center and the New York Marathon support Fred's Team, which was created in his honor. Special races raise money that supports cancer research efforts at Sloan-Kettering. These runners run for a cause — a cause that might one day help save lives.

It's true that there are negative things around us. It's an unfortunate fact of life. But Fred Lebow didn't let that stop him from creating a monster: a friendly monster called the New York Marathon that helps raise money and awareness for cancer.

We have to look at the other side of the equation: there are many ordinary people who do extraordinary things. Extraordinary things, that in Fred Lebow's case, will bring money and hope to many people with cancer. We hope one day there will be a cure. But for now, Mr. Lebow's legacy continues to make a life-saving difference in the race against cancer.